Richbaub's Introduction to Middle School Grammar Book 2

a Foundation in Grammar for Middle School Writers

by R. M. Gieson

First Edition

© 2016 Richard M. Gieson, Jr.

Richbaub's Ink Works

Cover Image Credit: © Mike Gieson - www.gieson.com

dedicated to

*Tracey, Alex, Will, and Kate, the happy background noise of
this project*

Support materials for this student workbook, including teacher's answer book and test booklet, are available for download at

www.middleschoolgrammar.com.

Introduction

I am not a grammar fanatic. I began to work on what would eventually become *Richbaub's Introduction to Middle School Grammar* because I wanted to create more time for reading and writing in my classes at a school that had a big fat grammar strand in its English curriculum. It's true.

I was previously always known as "the writing guy" because of all the writing my students did. My students produced writing magazines, I started the school newspaper, my classes soared on standardized writing tests. But that was then. Of course, now I'm "the grammar guy"... and it's all because I wanted to write more. It's all very ironic. I let them say what they will, but my main interest and my main strength remains and always will be teaching kids how to write well—it's just that I consider *Richbaub's* a very important part of my writing program, and I hope you come to feel this way, too!

The foundational beliefs behind *Richbaub's Introduction to Middle School Grammar* are:

1. Grammar instruction is an important part of a writing curriculum.

2. A grammar strand must be a proper, manageable, and appropriate size.

3. Quality grammar instruction requires some "decontextualized" lessons and practice, yet a grammar program should constantly remind and show students how an awareness of grammatical concepts can be applied to improving one's speaking and writing, most specifically one's <u>academic</u> speaking and writing.

*   *   *

More than a decade ago I arrived at a middle school where grammar, plus usage and mechanics, was an unusually large component of the English program. This was something new to me.

Up until that point in my teaching career, the driving forces of the middle school English programs I'd experienced were things like reading and writing workshops, literature circles (book clubs), interdisciplinary learning, and the six traits of writing. The formal teaching of grammar, usage, and mechanics (GU&M), it seemed, had slipped in stature and been marginalized. Grammar felt like something one maybe ought to teach, but not too much—maybe 5-10% of a student's grade would be comprised of GU&M assignments and evaluations, if it were factored into the grade book at all.

My new teaching post at, let's call it "Traditional Middle School," where I was assigned to teach sixth and eighth grade English, had so much GU&M in the curriculum that GU&M was making up 30% or more of students' grades in English. There were GU&M textbooks and workbooks—lots of GU&M taught the old-fashioned "drill and kill" way. Between this heavy GU&M load and my having only taught GU&M in dribs and drabs, something had to give!

To make a long and sometimes contentious story short, a few things happened during my nine-year stay at Traditional Middle School.

First, I learned a lot of grammar! As a result, my eyes were opened to what a dependable teaching tool grammar can be for presenting rules in usage and mechanics. For instance, when teaching good comma usage, it is easier when students can identify introductory elements like prepositional phrases, subordinate clauses, and verbal phrases. Understanding the parts of a sentence comes in handy when punctuating compound sentences or when discussing fragments and run-on sentences. In addition, teaching agreement, pronoun usage, or even, say, the difference between *well* and *good* is simplified if students have a solid foundation of grammatical knowledge and, therefore, share with their teacher a common grammatical vocabulary.

Most importantly, however, I discovered grammar's usefulness in communicating with students about writing style. During revision, I would encourage students to see how often they'd begun sentences with prepositional phrases and to strive for variety in sentence beginnings by adding in an introductory subordinate clause or participial phrase. Perhaps they could move a subject <u>after</u> the verb in a sentence. I could explain a fragment by stating that a sentence must be a complete thought <u>and</u> have a subject and a verb. I could explain weak verb choice by telling students to be aware of not depending too much on linking verbs. I could ask students to remove unnecessary helping verbs. In the pursuit of longer sentences, sentence combining through the use of subordinate clauses and verbal (participial, gerund, and infinitive) phrases could be easily articulated. **It's just much easier to guide students to analyze, experiment with, and improve their own writing styles when they have a good foundation in grammar.**

Some people want their students, as a result of studying grammar, to begin to think grammatically when composing sentences, but that's not the point of teaching grammar. Granted, while you're writing there are some tricky situations grammar can help you through at certain moments like, for instance, agreement or whether to use *me* or *I*, but generally when you're writing, your thoughts are dominated by ideas, not things like spelling, grammar, and mechanics. The ideas must flow unimpeded!

But during the revision process, GU&M knowledge helps you to correctly insert or delete commas, to evaluate your verb usage, to vary sentence patterns, etc., all of those finer things that lead to a clean, polished, and impressive final draft.

In addition, I like what the National Council for Teachers of English (NCTE) had to say about the question "Why Is Grammar Important?":

> "Grammar is important because it is the language that makes it possible for us to talk about language. Grammar names the types of words and word groups that make up sentences not only in English but in any language…

> "People associate grammar with errors and correctness. But *knowing about* grammar also helps us understand what makes sentences and paragraphs clear and interesting and precise. Grammar can be part of literature discussions, when we and our students closely read the sentences in poetry and stories. And *knowing about* grammar means finding out that all languages and all dialects follow grammatical patterns." *(source: NCTE's Assembly for the Teaching of English Grammar, 2002)*

Simply put, spending the time to give students a substantial foundation in grammar is essential if you're planning to lead students to be as proficient in the English language as they can be. Ignoring a formal instruction of grammar during the middle school years is a mistake!

But Don't Kids Need to *Write* to Become Better Writers, Rather Than Sit Through Grammar Lessons?

Actually, the research tells us that the number one thing a person can do to become a better writer is to <u>read</u>! This struck me as counterintuitive at first, but it makes a lot of sense when you think about it this way: We learn by taking things in. Sitting down and writing is not taking things in; writing is output, not input.

Steven Krashen champions this idea in a small part of his book *The Power of Reading: Insights from the Research* (second edition, 2004). Citing numerous studies, Krashen summarizes:

"More writing does not necessarily lead to better writing. Although some studies show that good writers do more writing than poor writers, increasing the amount of writing students do does not increase their writing proficiency" (135).

Reading, on the other hand, is so important to the process of becoming a better writer because through the process of reading, one is constantly fed good grammar, good writing, and interesting techniques and styles.

Writing has a higher purpose: Writing helps us think through things, or, as Krashen puts it: "Writing can help us solve problems and make us smarter" (132). Writing is thinking, and so writing is invaluable in the pursuit of knowledge and therefore invaluable to anyone who wants to become a better thinker.

There recently was a lot of hubbub about "writing across the curriculum," and this was a terrific idea, but not, as was suggested (and commonly believed), because more writing would improve students' writing skills. Rather, writing in math class would help students better think through math problems. Writing in science would help students increase the quality of their thinking about science topics, etc. In other words, the activity of writing would improve students' thinking, not necessarily their writing.

With the reading and writing workshop movement afoot over the last couple of decades, many students are doing a whole lot of writing, squeezing out time for "inputting" things like GU&M and vocabulary, which are taught only in tiny bits and pieces through "mini lessons."

The reason for all of the writing is based on a false analogy that goes like this: Practicing something makes you better at that something. For instance, when you practice playing tennis you become a better tennis player. Therefore, it certainly must follow that practicing writing will make you a better writer.

There actually is research that concludes that doing more reading will make you a better reader. As summarized by Krashen, research has shown that kids who read a lot over the summer make greater gains in their reading ability than students who do little or no reading over the summer, that students who read the most in their free time make the most gains in reading achievement, etc. etc. etc. (8-9).

The research about improving one's writing, however, is quite different. Again citing numerous studies, Krashen makes it plain: "We do not learn to write by writing… Language acquisition comes from input, not output, from comprehension, not production" (133, 136).

For developing writers, writing certainly allows students to practice what they have learned about good writing, but, again, writing in and of itself does not improve one's writing.

Sometimes I hear teachers encouraged to work to increase their students' "writing stamina" by having them write for longer and longer time periods, but that philosophy 1.) ignores the research about how to improve one's writing and 2.) consumes learning time that would more wisely be spent presenting information about writing for the students to take in.

Especially for developing writers, in addition to reading, studying the language in depth (i.e. learning new words, studying the language's grammar, usage, and mechanics), studying writing exemplars, and studying writing techniques and styles are all more important than constant writing practice!

Now, what gets ugly about the "grammar wars" is that even if you think teaching grammar is important, and most everyone does, not many people agree on how best to feed this knowledge to our students, so let me just say that the GU&M instruction that students receive through *Richbaub's Introduction to Middle School Grammar* (*Richbaub's IMSG*) is unique!

Richbaub's IMSG is not over simplified, nor is it overstuffed. Most importantly, *Richbaub's IMSG* has a constant ear to how the application of grammatical concepts relates to improving one's writing, and the practice exercises you will find in *Richbaub's IMSG* —which often involve sentence composition—are not divorced from writing. Finally, the topics covered within the *Richbaub's IMSG* program have been selected because of their practicality for developing writers at the middle school level as well as for their foundational significance to higher-level GU&M concepts to which students will soon be exposed.

Why So Oppositional?

For some reason, grammar instruction and writing instruction have an oppositional relationship in many teachers' minds. Stereotypical grammar fans are all about drill and kill and they do little actual writing. Stereotypical writing workshop fans abhor grammar and so their students just write, baby! But grammar is actually an important part of a good writing program, not the enemy of one.

As an analogy, I think about cooking. It's certainly possible to become a good cook just by making things in the kitchen over and over. You can become quite proficient simply through your hands-on experiences if you have any talent at all. So what would formal training in the "culinary arts" add to your skills? What if you enriched your knowledge by studying a little agriculture as it relates to food, or the cultural influences on your favorite dishes, or the chemistry behind the reactions taking place in the kitchen or on the palette, or the techniques of some expert chefs? Your understanding would enlarge your culinary toolbox and help refine your skills. Similarly, an understanding of grammar enlarges a writer's toolbox and helps refine his or her language skills, just as studying literature and learning vocabulary also enhance a writer's skills.

This special knowledge about the language does not <u>control</u> writing skill, and so it's certainly true that skill with grammar does not necessarily equate to writing skill. But an understanding of grammar must be in place if we are to give our students a chance to become *expert* writers.

The final realization I came to about teaching grammar in middle school during my time at Traditional Middle School was that there's only so much GU&M a student and a curriculum should be asked to absorb—for both practical and developmental reasons. Yes, we still do want to keep actual writing activities at the forefront of writing instruction, which means that a grammar program must be of the appropriate scale. A grammar program cannot, for instance, be so large that it chokes out time for a sufficient amount of reading and writing!

But have you ever noticed how difficult it is to find a GU&M program that seems to have seriously considered both the developmental level of students and the fact that there are other things to teach besides GU&M? This puzzling situation certainly was another major force behind the creation of *Richbaub's Introduction to Middle School Grammar*.

Taking a Long View

The development of *Richbaub's IMSG*, which includes topics in usage and mechanics as well, was a process that began not only with the practical realizations mentioned above, but also by taking aim at where students, as writers, have the potential to be at the end of their middle school years.

For instance, in the writing of the most-driven and most-talented 15-year olds, it is evident that they are able to consciously tap into their GU&M knowledge to improve their writing styles as well as to meet the technical requirements of academic writing. They understand what a subordinate clause is, and they can begin a thesis statement with one if you ask them to—and they know to follow the clause with a comma! When you write "comma splice" in the margin, these students know what you mean. They can recognize problems with parallel structure, too. Their writing has a mix of complex and simple sentences, and they work to sometimes begin with a participial phrase. In addition, they are cognizant of pronoun case usage rules, the rules of agreement, and how modifiers can be misplaced. These students also recognize active voice writing and will work to limit their use of helping and linking verbs.

Certainly, I'm not talking about mastery here; it's probably impossible to become an expert writer in one's teens! What I am talking about is what 15-year olds (8th-9th graders) are capable of, developmentally speaking, when it comes to turning GU&M knowledge into a useful tool to improve their writing (and speaking, too!)

And so when you consider what 15-year olds are capable of doing when it comes to engaging GU&M knowledge to improve the way they communicate, you wonder about what kind of foundational knowledge they should be fed in the years preceding. i.e. When a ninth-grade teacher sets out to discuss verbal phrases or sentence types—or any other advanced grammar concept students are now developmentally ready to handle—what prior knowledge should already be in place?

The Quandary of the Farsighted Middle School English/Language Arts Teacher

When communicating about writing, high school teachers frequently use grammatical terms with their students, terms like fragment, subordinate clause, misplaced modifier, preposition, conjunction, pronoun usage, run on, etc. A true understanding of such things requires a background in grammar.

Middle school is the most obvious place to deliver this background information, but there are some very big problems middle school teachers face:

1.) Traditional middle school grammar programs are gargantuan, and thus they consume way too much teaching time.

2.) Paring down a large grammar program to better fit into today's heavy reading and writing-focused curricula is a very complicated thing (ask anyone who's tried), and it's virtually impossible for an experienced, strong-minded English department to do so collectively.

3.) Current trends, therefore, favor teaching grammar with only intermittent grammar mini-lessons. A mini lesson here and a mini lesson there is a rather haphazard way to build a foundation in anything to support more advanced learning in the years ahead. The mini lesson approach for teaching grammar, more often than not, also leaves teachers scrambling to create their own lessons and lesson materials, especially if a teacher is interested in any kind of sustained teaching of important grammar concepts throughout a school year.

Good news: *Richbaub's IMSG* has been created to solve these problems for middle school teachers!

Developing a Quality Middle School Grammar Program

Once the importance of the study of GU&M has been acknowledged and the end-of-middle-school goals have been established regarding how GU&M instruction should begin to manifest itself in students' writing, teachers of rising middle school students must decide how to approach GU&M. How much time can teachers allot to GU&M in light of the fact that they are also charged with not only studying other aspects of writing, as well as literature and vocabulary, but also (in many schools) with carving out time for students to read independently? Which GU&M topics should be covered and in what sequence? Which topics do not require formal study? Which topics should be left for future study?

During my tenure at Traditional Middle School this decision-making process resulted in the origins of *Richbaub's IMSG*. It was an on-the-ground, trial-and-error process inside my sixth and eighth-grade English classrooms.

Richbaub's IMSG, building on the basic grammar taught at the elementary level, completes students' foundation in rudimentary grammar. The parts of speech are reviewed, sentence parts are learned, problematic topics in mechanics are covered, and then this knowledge is applied toward developing an understanding of proper usage and improved writing style.

In addition, *Richbaub's IMSG* very clearly communicates to students that the study of grammar is all about writing, i.e. understanding the English language's patterns and components and practicing putting words together in the clearest and most effective way. Throughout *Richbaub's IMSG*, students compose sentences employing various structures and grammatical components, and improving one's writing is the specific focus of several sections of the program.

Ultimately, *Richbaub's IMSG*'s job is to provide a foundation in grammar for middle school writers—a foundation of "formal training" upon which students can stand and stretch upward toward their fullest potentials as writers in the months and years ahead!

It's Not About Mastery So Much as It's About Thinking!

Something also must be said about the <u>push</u> of grammar on the intellect of middle school students.

For maybe the first time, students will be confronted with concepts that they don't easily "get." They are going to have to think hard, contemplate, listen closely, consider, and analyze—things that they're really not used to having to do day in and day out.

In other words, grammar is a challenge that forces students to really think!

Why is "really thinking" so tough for middle school students? Because of where they are developmentally, or, in my experience, where they've just recently arrived developmentally. Middle school students are only just pulling into the advanced reasoning "station," so to speak.

Teaching grammar is not just about better writing and better speaking; grammar also involves the development of thinking that is more abstract, more methodical, more structured, and more logical— advanced things that are just coming into reach for middle school students.

Entering middle school, students are accustomed, <u>generally speaking</u>, to demonstrating their learning in the language arts through tasks that require memorizing, being creative, reporting, and summarizing— things very developmentally appropriate at the elementary level.

Applying grammar concepts, on the other hand, often requires methodical and critical reasoning. Things need to be figured out, contemplated, considered, handled in a disciplined, step-by-step fashion, and often weighed carefully before an answer can be settled on.

In other words, grammar helps middle school students to prod new intellectual levels. Some students will struggle with this more than others, but all students will be forced to reach toward new heights in their thinking.

Anyone teaching grammar to middle school kids will quickly realize that applying strategies and orderly analysis to, for instance, determining if a verb is an action verb or a linking verb, is a mighty struggle for many students. If this, then that. Size up the situation. Match it to a pattern. Make a determination <u>after</u> the application of taught strategies. They are not used to such structured thinking!

Verbs can be particularly challenging, for instance. Helping verbs, main verbs, verb phrases, action and linking verbs… Lots of puzzled looks. Lots of confusion.

Try this: Show students a few different ways they can decide if a verb is action or linking. Then give them a sentence like this:

At the party last night Mary Beth looked very tired.

Ask students if the verb *looked* is an action verb or a linking verb. When the first student answers, ask him to explain his thinking, i.e. how he decided what kind of verb, linking or action, *looked* is. In this situation, I very rarely hear a student explain how he applied one of the strategies presented beforehand. Usually, it turns out that he fell back on a sort of gut feeling or first impression about the verb in question.

When faced with a situation that requires some real analysis, many students look for simple, "homemade" solutions instead. They guess or make up half-baked ways of thinking to handle what seems overwhelming. They do not know how to analyze or how to apply strategies, for they haven't had much experience doing so because the part of their mind that handles this kind of thinking is still developing. Teachers can "walk them through," but it's very difficult for students to put aside their urges, assumptions, and "the first thing that pops into their minds" and, instead, apply new thinking strategies.

Here's another example. Tell students about nominative case and objective case personal pronouns and how, in the subject position of a sentence, they may only use *nominative* case personal pronouns.

Follow up by giving students ten sentences where they have to choose the correct pronoun to use in a subject position, such as:

(Me, I) and my dad flew to Alaska to camp and fish for a week.

In reviewing their work, you will find that more than a few students have selected pronouns based on what <u>sounds</u> correct to them (*me*), ignoring the information about using only nominative case personal pronouns in the subject position (they should select *I*).

These kinds of experiences can cause problems for teachers. Some teachers give up teaching any challenging grammar. Others will spend exorbitant amounts of time re-teaching. These are common reactions and common mistakes.

In order to successfully teach grammar in middle school, a teacher needs to understand that teaching grammar is not really about students mastering every important grammar concept (impossible!), but rather 1.) planting an awareness of and some skill with grammar and 2.) stretching and expanding students' thinking skills.

Many things taught in the language arts in middle school are like this, from literary analysis to multi-paragraph essay writing. Students are being <u>introduced</u> to new knowledge and new ways of thinking, and it's hoped that they will gain not necessarily mastery (that's unrealistic given students' developmental levels), but a <u>foundation</u> of skills and knowledge on which future, more advanced learning can be built.

With these things in mind, throughout the *Richbaub's* program key concepts are constantly reviewed in a very cumulative way. It's very different from the "mini lesson" approach where a concept is taught and then too rarely, or perhaps never, revisited. In addition, the program's evaluations, although challenging, do not demand too much from students as many traditional grammar programs' tests have a tendency to do.

After *Richbaub's IMSG*

Post-*Richbaub's IMSG*, students will have a foundation in grammar that will help them meet any challenge dealing with the nuts and bolts of the English language. For teachers, *Richbaub's IMSG* secures a context for all future references to and lessons in grammatical things, whether they are additional topics selected from a traditional GU&M text, to more immersive activities like sentence combining, to lessons in grammar woven into writing workshop activities, to even an as-needed, remedial approach to teaching GU&M.

Conclusion

Teachers often want to jump past such things as teaching the parts of speech or parsing action and linking verbs. How old fashioned! How dull! But try to explain fragments to high school students by discussing subjects and verbs, and you'll only get a sea of blank faces! Get into a discussion about good verb usage, and, um, what's that, Tommy? "What's a *linking* verb?" How do you begin to explain such a thing to students to whom no one's ever taken the time to teach grammar? And exactly how does one teach students the difference between *me* and *I* without mentioning prepositional phrases, subjects, or complements? Etc., etc., etc.

My point is that if you want your students to <u>really</u> understand the language, you must lay the groundwork, and that means taking the time to teach some grammar.

Unfortunately, well-meaning teachers find it difficult to properly scale a grammar strand to fit into their curriculum... And so they give up. It is nearly <u>impossible</u> to find a manageable or sensible way to trim down the content of textbooks focused on grammar.

But that's exactly what *Richbaub's IMSG* is designed to do!

Once again, *Richbaub's IMSG* provides a foundation in grammar for middle school writers—a foundation of "formal training" upon which students can stand and stretch up toward their fullest potentials as writers in the months and years ahead!

No matter where your students are headed after *Richbaub's IMSG*, you can be sure that they have received content that is suitable in scale, rich in content, and appropriate to their developmental level.

And for teachers, *Richbaub's IMSG* is the grammar strand you've been looking for as it fits seamlessly beside the literature, writing, and vocabulary study in today's middle school English classrooms.

Welcome to *Richbaub's IMSG*!

Table of Contents

Chapter 1

Prepositions, Nouns, Pronouns, & Verbs (part 1)

Terms to know:

Preposition
Prepositional phrase
Object of the preposition (o.p.)
Conjunction

Noun
Pronoun
Personal pronoun
Objective case personal pronouns
Nominative case personal pronouns

Infinitive
Helping verb
Main verb
Verb phrase
Single-word verb
Polluted verb phrase

SCHOLAR ZONE: HOW MUCH DO YOU KNOW ABOUT THE ENGLISH LANGUAGE?

The English alphabet we use today was influenced by an ancient alphabet called the "Runic" alphabet. The Runic alphabet was invented in the northern regions of Europe long before the English language was born.

Below, under each Runic letter is the letter you know that matches the sound represented by the Runic letter.

Runic   ᚠ ᛒ ᛣ ᛗ ᛗ ᚠ ᚷ ᚺ ᛁ   ᛃ ᛚ ᛗ ᚿ ᚠ ᚷ   ᚱ ᛥ ᛐ ᚠ   ᛈ ᛉ ᛇ ᛋ ᚠ ᛟ ᛏ ᛉ ᚦ ᛝ
Modern English A B C D E F G H I J K L M N O P Q R S T U V W X Y Z

Do you see any similarities between Runic and Modern English letters?

Warning... Super Scholar Zone!:

How come there are no Runic letters for "J" or "V"?

What do you think those extra Runic letters are for?

1.1 – Prepositions & Prepositional Phrases

Prepositions and prepositional phrases are everywhere! Knowing about them will help you immensely when analyzing the parts of a sentence. A good understanding of prepositional phrases will also help advance your writing skills because there are comma and pronoun usage rules associated with prepositional phrases. In addition, advanced writing concepts like agreement, sentence variety, and parallel structure are easier to understand when you know about prepositional phrases. Are you ready? Let's go!

A. **Prepositions** are words that <u>begin little phrases</u> that describe something's or someone's location in space or time (*in* the cupboard, *with* Janie, *above* the house, *after* the movie). These little phrases are called **prepositional phrases**.

B. Here is a list of forty of the most commonly-used prepositions:

about	below	in	out
above	beneath	in front of	over
across	beside	inside	through
after	between	instead of	to
against	beyond	into	toward
along	by	near	under
around	down	next to	until
at	during	of	up
before	for	off	with
behind	from	on	without

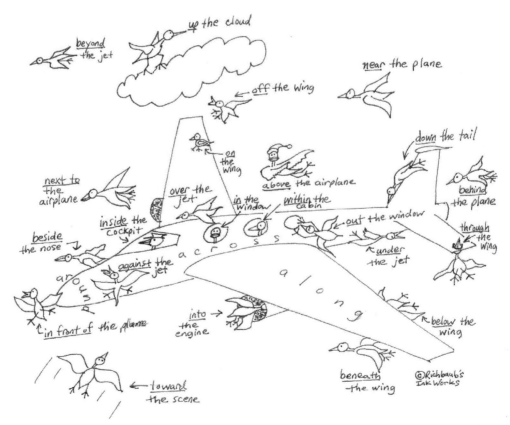

C. A **prepositional phrase** begins with a preposition and ends with a noun or pronoun.

D. In between the preposition and the noun or pronoun, there may be one or more descriptive words (adjectives and/or adverbs).

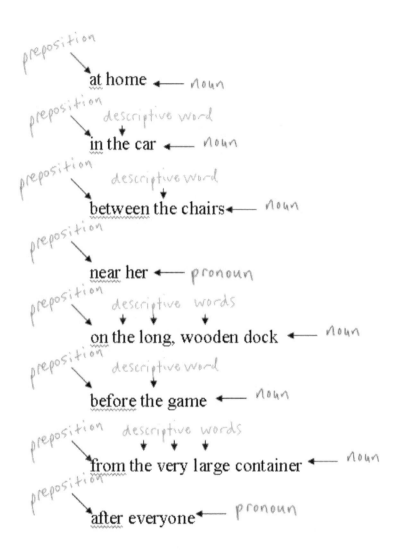

E. The <u>last</u> word in a prepositional phrase (the noun or pronoun that completes the phrase) is called the **object of the preposition**, or **"o.p."** for short.

F. In the examples above, the objects of the prepositions are: *home, car, chairs, her, dock, game, container* and *everyone*.

 **Exercise 1**

Part 1: Write your own prepositional phrases. Choose at least one preposition from each column in the "Prepositions Cheat Box."

1. _____   4. _____

2. _____   5. _____

3. _____   6. _____

Prepositions Cheat Box

about	below	in	out
above	beneath	in front of	over
across	beside	inside	through
after*	between	instead of	to
against	beyond	into	toward
along	by	near	under
around	down	next to	until*
at	during	of	up
before*	for	off	with
behind	from	on	without

Part 2: Surround prepositional phrases with parentheses in the following sentences. Only one sentence has more than one prepositional phrase.

7. I write with a pencil.

8. On Tuesday I must go home.

9. My grandfather should be sitting in the kitchen.

10. During the movie I ate popcorn with her.

11. Inside the cabinet you can find my books.

12. Before dinner I want to jog five miles.

BEWARE THE FAKE ONE!!

Do you remember what an *infinitive* is? HINT: *to* + a verb

Infinitives look like prepositional phrases…but they are NOT prepositional phrases!! They are verb forms. *Remember?*

#12 has an infinitive in it. Watch out!

Part 3: In the sentences above, circle the objects of the prepositions.

* Students will sometimes have trouble with these prepositions. See appendix for explanation.

Multiple Objects of Prepositions

A. Once in a while, you see a prepositional phrase that has two or three objects. For example:

prep.   noun   noun
from my mom and dad ⎯ objects of preposition

prep.   noun   noun
behind the sofa and lounge chair ⎯ objects of preposition

prep.   pronoun   pronoun
with him or her ⎯ objects of preposition

prep.   noun   noun   noun
over the cotton sheets, blankets and foam pillows ⎯ objects of preposition

prep.   noun   noun
in front of the older women and children ⎯ objects of preposition

✱ note: "and" & "or" are connecting words called conjunctions

Quick Practice: Write your own prepositional phrases that have <u>multiple objects</u>. Do NOT use any of the prepositions used above.

1. _____

2. _____

Above, circle the **conjunctions** (the connecting words) in each prepositional phrase.

SCHOLAR ZONE

During the time of the Roman Empire and before the birth of the English language, Romans came to England, or "Britain" as they called it. With them, the Romans brought the alphabet of their Latin language.

Here's the alphabet the Romans brought to England in the first century AD (CE):

Roman Latin   A B C D E F G H I L M N O P Q R S T V X Y Z

The Roman Latin alphabet has fewer letters than our modern English alphabet. **What are the missing letters and sounds?**

 **Exercise 2**

Part 1: In your own words, write a definition for each of the following terms:

Preposition: _____

_____

Prepositional phrase: _____

_____

Object of the preposition (o.p.): _____

_____

Conjunction: _____

_____

Part 2: Surround prepositional phrases with parentheses in the following sentences. Some sentences have more than one prepositional phrase.

1. The water below the bridge is moving fast.

2. With three friends I went on a hike in the mountains.

3. The subway train screeched to a halt at the station.

4. Jeffery has chosen the red bicycle beside the blue one.

5. I pulled off the road in front of the gas station to rest.

6. This tunnel was cut through the mountain in the 1980's.

7. At the concert I sat between Rosie and Bella.

8. I just finished a book about two brothers who lived on a houseboat.

about
above
across
after
against
along
around
at
before
behind
below
beneath
beside
between
beyond
by
down
during
for
from
in
in front of
inside
instead of
into
near
next to
of
off
on
out
over
through
to
toward
under
until
up
with
without

1.2 – Nouns & Pronouns

Armed with a sound knowledge of nouns and pronouns, you will be more skilled at telling where a prepositional phrase ends as well as better able to identify subjects in a sentence, which is something coming up in Chapter 2. Advanced writing concepts are also linked to an understanding of nouns and pronouns, things like when to use "I" vs. when instead to use "me," how subject-verb agreement works, and how using concrete nouns can improve the detail and imagery in your writing.

A. A **noun** is the most basic part of speech in the universe. Nouns are the words we use for the people, places, things, and ideas all around us, words like *boat, freedom, Africa, fork, grass, pencil,* etc.

B. **Pronouns** are a close cousin to nouns. Pronouns are alternate words we use for people, places, things, and ideas. For instance, in place of the nouns Joe and Mary, you might instead simply use the pronoun *they.* Instead of saying the noun *box,* you could use the pronoun *it.*

C. As you can see, although pronouns are used for the same kinds of things as nouns (people, places, things, and ideas), pronouns are not as specific as nouns.

D. One reason pronouns exist, however, is to provide us some variety.

E. Here's what a world without pronouns might sound like:

> *"Bob and Mabel were married after Bob got out of the Navy. Bob flew Navy jets. Bob was 18 when Bob met Mabel, but Bob didn't have the courage to ask Mabel to marry Bob until Bob turned 25, so Bob and Mabel dated for over seven years before Bob and Mabel got married."*

With pronouns you can refer to someone named Bob as *he* or *him* or someone named Mabel as *she* or *her* once in a while instead of saying their specific names all of the time. Isn't that just wonderful?

F. There are several types of pronouns, but the most important pronouns to know about, and also the most commonly used pronouns, are **personal pronouns**.

Personal Pronoun Usage Inside Prepositional Phrases

A. There are two main types of personal pronouns. One kind can NEVER be used in a prepositional phrase.

Objective Case Personal Pronouns	Nominative Case Personal Pronouns
me	I
you	you
her	she
it	it
him	he
us	we
them	they
*whom	*who

As you can see, *you* and *it* are objective <u>and</u> nominative case personal pronouns. They are "all-purpose" personal pronouns.

*Technically, *whom* and *who* are <u>not</u> personal pronouns. However, they behave exactly like personal pronouns, and so we are going to consider them to be personal pronouns from here on out! See appendix.

*There is also a <u>third</u> case of personal pronouns, the "possessive case." See appendix.

B. When using Personal Pronouns as objects of prepositions, you MUST choose an Objective Case Personal Pronoun. Get it? OBJECTIVE case for OBJECTS of the preposition?

C. In other words...**The words *I*, *she*, *he*, *we*, *they*, and *who* can NEVER be used in prepositional phrases!!**

Examples:

CORRECT: John went fishing (with me and my dad).
"...with my dad and I" would be <u>incorrect</u>

INCORRECT: (To my mom and I), chocolate is a wonderful thing.
"To me and my mom" would be <u>correct</u>

INCORRECT: They sat (near Bill and I).
"...near me and Bill" would be <u>correct</u>

CORRECT: This magazine article is (about him and Sam).
"...about he and Sam" would be <u>incorrect</u>

Exercise 3

You will need to use Personal Pronouns for this exercise:

Personal Pronoun Refresher Box

Objective Case Personal Pronouns	Nominative Case Personal Pronouns
me	I
you	you
her	she
it	it
him	he
us	we
them	they
whom	who

As you can see, *you* and *it* are objective <u>and</u> nominative case personal pronouns. They are "all-purpose" pronouns!

Part 1: Write prepositional phrases that begin with the given letters and…

have a personal pronoun for each object of the preposition (o.p.)

1. t _____

2. i _____

3. a _____

each have <u>two</u> personal pronoun o.p.'s.

4. n _____

5. b _____

6. w _____

Mistakes with personal pronouns inside prepositional phrases are common <u>when there are two or more o.p.'s</u>.

That is the situation to be very careful about!

Part 2: Circle only the <u>correct</u> prepositional phrases:

7. between he and I

8. for Jim and me

9. for me and them

10. to me

11. from you and her

12. to who

13. beneath whom

14. with she

15. with him

16. to you and I

about
above
across
after
against
along
around
at
before
behind
below
beneath
beside
between
beyond
by
down
during
for
from
in
in front of
inside
instead of
into
near
next to
of
off
on
out
over
through
to
toward
under
until
up
with
without

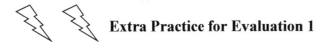 **Extra Practice for Evaluation 1**

Part 1: Write two **original** prepositional phrases. Each prepositional phrase should have only ONE object of the preposition (o.p.)

1. _____

2. _____

Part 2: Write one **original** prepositional phrase that has multiple objects. Do NOT use any of the prepositions used above.

3. _____

Part 3: Surround prepositional phrases with parentheses in the following sentences, **AND** circle the objects of the prepositions (o.p.'s) in each prepositional phrase.

Example: I threw the ball (over the (fence)).

4. In July we pitched our tents in a pine forest near the highway.

5. I called from my neighbor's phone.

6. The message about the party did not reach Melanie on time.

7. We sat in the courtyard with Doug and Jill in the shadow of Mount

Kilimanjaro.

about
above
across
after
against
along
around
at
before
behind
below
beneath
beside
between
beyond
by
down
during
for
from
in
in front of
inside
instead of
into
near
next to
of
off
on
out
over
through
to
toward
under
until
up
with
without

Part 4: In your own words, write a definition for the following term:

Object of the Preposition (o.p.): _____

_____

Personal Pronoun Refresher Box

Objective Case Personal Pronouns	Nominative Case Personal Pronouns
me	I
you	you
her	she
it	it
him	he
us	we
them	they
whom	who

As you can see, *you* and *it* are objective <u>and</u> nominative case personal pronouns. They are "all-purpose" pronouns!

Part 5: Circle only the <u>completely correct</u> prepositional phrases:

8. with Billy and he

9. between my dad and I

10. over me

11. toward she and him

12. between me and him

13. for I

14. in front of we and they

15. from us and them

16. next to she

> *Mistakes with personal pronouns inside prepositional phrases are common <u>when there are two or more o.p.'s</u>.*
>
> **That** is the situation to be very careful about!

BTW: There <u>will</u> be a "Prepositions Cheat Box" <u>and</u> a "Personal Pronoun Refresher Box" on the evaluation.

 Evaluation 1: A Review of Prepositions & Prepositional Phrases, Nouns & Pronouns, and Personal Pronoun Usage in Prepositional Phrases

SCHOLAR ZONE

Pun Fun

A pun is a humorous comment or joke based on the similarities between words and/or the double meanings of words and phrases. Here are some puns:

> I wondered why the baseball was getting bigger; then it hit me.

Above, "it hit me" has a literal meaning, as if the ball actually slammed into the author's face. But "it hit me" also has a figurative meaning—it is also something people say when they suddenly realize something. Do you think this is funny? If not, you probably aren't alone. Some people think puns are pretty lame attempts at humor, but they are one popular way people play around with language.

Here are some more puns:

> Why did the golfer bring an extra set of pants? In case he got a hole in one.

> When a clock is hungry it goes back four seconds.

> The guy who fell into the upholstery machine was fully recovered.

Do you know any puns?

Pun
Fun

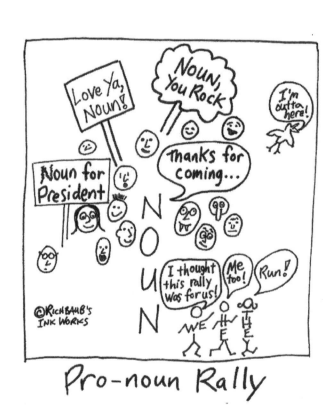

Pro-noun Rally

1.3 – Verbs, part 1

Many times, the key to improving a sentence lies in improving the sentence's verb. A better verb can improve a sentence's clarity as well as its imagery, and paying attention to the placement of verbs plays a role in having better sentence variety.

Therefore, a grammatical understanding of verbs is a very powerful thing to possess—it's one of the advantages expert writers have over average writers. Experts' verb knowledge includes knowing the difference between action and linking verbs, understanding helping verbs, and being able to discern the difference between active and passive voice writing. If you pay close attention, you too can possess this special knowledge!

A. Every sentence has at least one verb. Verbs generally explain what the subject of a sentence is doing, or they state that the subject is being something. Below, the verbs are underlined:

I <u>leaped</u> up onto the boulder.

We <u>had stayed</u> in Maine for three days.

My cousin in California <u>surfs</u> in the Pacific Ocean.

Those people <u>are being</u> very loud!

B. **A Special Verb Form: The Infinitive**
Before you put a verb into a certain tense or pair it with a subject, verbs are in a form called the "infinitive form." The infinitive form of a verb looks a lot like a prepositional phrase—but it's NOT a prepositional phrase!

C. Here's a verb in the infinitive form: **to cook**. Here's another: **to sing**. So the infinitive form is *to* plus a verb.

D. Verbs in the infinitive form are never *THE* verb in a sentence. In other words, the infinitive is never the thing the subject of the sentence is doing. Below, *THE* verb is underlined:

She <u>likes</u> **to cook** on weekends.

(She is <u>liking</u> something, not <u>cooking</u> something.)

The twins <u>want</u> **to have** a giant birthday party this year.

(The twins are <u>wanting</u> something, not <u>having</u> something.)

E. **Verbs have many different forms.** The infinitive form is just one form. Two other forms are the present tense and the past tense.

Here is an example of one verb's various forms:

infinitive	present tense			past tense	
to ask	base form	**ask:** "I ask," "We ask," etc.	"ed" form	**asked:** "I asked," "You asked," etc.	
	"s" form	**asks:** "She asks," "He asks," etc.			
	"ing" form	**asking:** "I <u>am</u> asking," etc.			

FAQ's:

F. What's the word *am* doing in there right above the arrow??

The word *am* is <u>helping</u> the verb work in this sentence. You couldn't say "I asking."

Actually, *am* has even become part of the verb. **The verb in this sentence would be "am asking."**

Other words we use to help verbs work include *was*, *be*, *were*, *can*, *may*, and many more! For example:

<u>was</u> asked   <u>were</u> asking   <u>can</u> ask   <u>may be</u> asking

G. What about the future tense??

To speak about doing something in the future, English requires you to use one or more <u>helping verbs</u>. For example:

She <u>**will**</u> **ask** you about your homework. *(The verb in this sentence is "will ask.")*

My brother <u>**will be**</u> **asking** you for a ride to school. *(The verb in this sentence is "will be asking.")*

Verb Phrases

A. Multiple-word verbs (or verbs that have helping verbs) are called "verb phrases," so a sentence may contain a single-word verb **OR** a verb phrase.

B. In a verb phrase the last word is the "main verb." The other words are "helping verbs." **The whole thing together is what you would call "the verb."**

Under the bridge Johnny *may be fishing* for trout.

> verb = may be fishing
> helping verbs = may, be
> main verb = fishing

Helping Verbs

The following words are always helping verbs:

would	will	may
could	can	might
should		must

This next set of words are also <u>often</u> helping verbs. However, they're *not* helping verbs *all* the time. Sometimes they are main verbs in a verb phrase or even verbs all by themselves (single-word verbs).

be	are	is	have	do
been	am	was	had	does
		were	has	did

*The *-ing* form of the verb *be* (*being*) also qualifies for this list but is omitted for the sake of simplicity. See appendix for a discussion of <u>participles, infinitives, and gerunds</u>.

SCHOLAR ZONE

The earliest speakers of what would become the English language were northern Europeans who invaded England in the 5th and 6th centuries AD (CE), after the Roman Empire collapsed. They were from various tribes, including the Angles, Saxons, Jutes, Franks, and Frisians, but we have come to refer to them generally as the "Anglo-Saxons."

English, or "Anglish," was a combination of the assorted Germanic languages these invaders spoke. English also eventually adopted the Latin alphabet the Romans had earlier brought to Britain. A new language had been born, a language with a Latin alphabet and heavy with Germanic words, but not nearly finished!

Over the next several hundred years, many new words would enter the language, and spellings and pronunciations would be adjusted. Old English would be very tough for a modern-day English speaker to read. Then came Middle English, and finally Modern English in the 16th century. Modern English has continued to evolve, but 16th century English, which is the English William Shakespeare used, can be read fairly easily by today's English speakers.

Warning... Scholar Zone!: Any idea how *England* got its name?

 **Exercise 4**

Part 1 (review): Circle the words below that you are <u>allowed</u> to use in a prepositional phrase. You may <u>circle one or more than one word in each line.</u>

1.	he	whom	him	I	she	me
2.	you	they	her	we	it	us

Part 2: In the line below each sentence, write out one part of the sentence as directed.

3. The military men met with the president to plan a strategy for the war.

   What's the <u>infinitive</u> in the above sentence? _____

4. At the end of the game the star player should have made that layup.

   What's the <u>verb</u> in the above sentence? _____

5. Thomas has never sat between Jennifer and me before.

   What's the <u>prepositional phrase</u> in the above sentence? _____

6. That missed field goal would have given my team the lead.

   Write the <u>helping verb(s)</u> from the above sentence: _____

7. John was being very rude during David's presentation yesterday.

   Write the <u>main verb</u> from the above sentence: _____

Part 3: In your own words, write a definition for each of the following terms:

8. Helping verb: _____

   _____

9. Infinitive: _____

   _____

10. Verb phrase: _____

    _____

11. Single-word verb: _____

    _____

12. Main verb: _____

    _____

"Polluted" Verb Phrases

A. In many verb phrases, there is a word hidden among the helping and main verbs that is not actually part of the verb phrase. When this occurs, you might say that the verb phrase is "polluted."

> **Example 1:** Mark <u>may</u> **not** <u>meet</u> us at the movie tonight.

B. In "pure" verb phrases, each word is a helping verb or a form of some verb.

> **Example 2:** In the attic six boxes <u>will be stacked</u> near the chimney.

C. When identifying verbs in sentences, never include "polluting" words. For instance, in "Example 1" above, the verb is "may meet." The word *not* is a polluting word and is not really part of the verb.

D. Here's a list of non-verbs that are often found between helping and main verbs:

(Do **not** include these in your verb phrases!)

not	almost
never	also
still	
already	<u>most</u> words ending in –ly, like *continually* and *quietly*

Note: These words are adverbs. We'll discuss adverbs later.

E. <u>Each word in a verb phrase must be a verb or a known helping verb</u>, so don't include other parts of speech in a verb phrase.

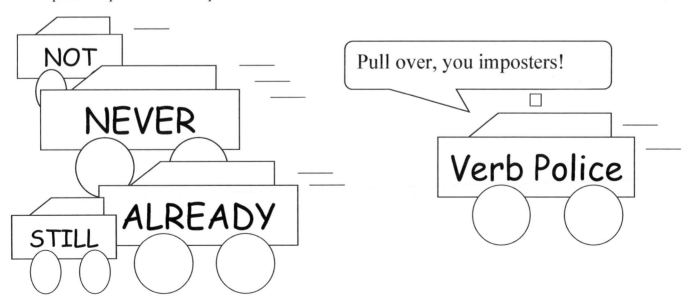

 **Exercise 5**

Directions: Underline the verbs and put parentheses around the prepositional phrases.

Example 1: (In my house) my sister <u>reads</u> (in the living room).

Example 2: A flock (of birds) <u>was flying</u> high (in the sky).

Example 3: The students <u>may <s>not</s> work</u> (in the library) (after school).

1. The children did not sit at their desks.

2. Around the edge of the lake the geese searched for a snack.

3. The cookies inside the box have melted in the summer heat.

4. My grandfather lives with my mom and me in our log cabin.

5. The grass next to the fence was growing very tall.

6. Those jets may fly in the air show on Saturday.

7. You will never see a polar bear in a rain forest!

about
above
across
after
against
along
around
at
before
behind
below
beneath
beside
between
beyond
by
down
during
for
from
in
in front of
inside
instead of
into
near
next to
of
off
on
out
over
through
to
toward
under
until
up
with
without

Helping Verb Refresher Box

The following words are always helping verbs:

would	will	may
could	can	might
should		must

This next set of words are also <u>often</u> helping verbs. However, they're *not* helping verbs *all* the time. Sometimes they are main verbs in a verb phrase or even verbs all by themselves (single-word verbs).

be	are	is	have	do
been	am	was	had	does
		were	has	did

Exercise 6

Part 1: In the blank after each sentence, write out the verb. If you find a verb phrase, <u>don't include non-verbs when you write out the verb!</u>

1. I may not be going to college soon. _____

2. In front of the house a tall tree created a huge patch of shade. _____

3. The boy between Mary and me might be sleeping. _____

4. The bus did arrive at the bus stop. _____

5. Mr. Riches is still teaching at Wonderwood Middle School. _____

6. Behind Thomas and her I could see three more people. _____

7. My mom went for a jog along the river walk. _____

8. I would never tell my parents a lie. _____

Part 2: Surround prepositional phrases with parentheses AND underline verbs. Watch out for verb phrases and polluting words, and remember that verbs can never be inside prepositional phrases.

9. Under the bridge I am feeding the lonely ducks.

10. The recycling bin has already been emptied by Tim.

11. During math class I dropped my pencil on the floor.

12. On the deck in my backyard a frog was croaking in the night.

about
above
across
after
against
along
around
at
before
behind
below
beneath
beside
between
beyond
by
down
during
for
from
in
in front of
inside
instead of
into
near
next to
of
off
on
out
over
through
to
toward
under
until
up
with
without

Helping Verb Refresher Box

The following words are always helping verbs:

would	will	may
could	can	might
should		must

This next set of words are also often helping verbs. However, they're *not* helping verbs *all* the time. Sometimes they are main verbs in a verb phrase or even verbs all by themselves (single-word verbs).

be	are	is	have	do
been	am	was	had	does
		were	has	did

 **Advanced Exercise**

Directions: Write an originally worded definition for at least five of the following terms. Write your definition in the format of a real dictionary entry.

Examples:

from www.vocabulary.com:

archipelago (ar-kah-PEL-ah-go) – 1.) A large group of islands. 2.) a sea, such as the Aegean Sea, containing a large number of scattered islands

from www.dictionary.com:

archipelago [ahr-k*uh*-pel-*uh*-goh] **noun, plural** archipelagos, archipelagoes.

1. a large group or chain of islands: *the Malay Archipelago.*

2. any large body of water with many islands.

Terms:

prepositional phrase _____

_____

object of the preposition (o.p) _____

_____

conjunction _____

_____

verb phrase _____

_____

infinitive _____

_____

helping verb _____

_____

main verb _____

_____

polluted verb phrase _____

_____

Extra Practice for Evaluation 2

Part 1: Circle the prepositional phrases below that are completely <u>correct</u>.

1. under him and her   with she   for me and my dad

2. to Chris and I   between he and her   toward her and me

3. over us and them   near Nina and they   by you and he

Part 2: In your own words, write a definition for each of the following terms:

4. helping verb _____

_____

5. main verb _____

_____

6. object of the preposition (o.p.) _____

_____

Part 3: Surround prepositional phrases with parentheses, and, in the blank after each sentence, write out the verb. If you find a verb phrase, <u>don't include non-verbs (polluting words) when you write out the verb</u>!

7. Peter would like to go on a trip to Austria. _____

8. The glasses were in that duffel bag near him and her. _____

9. After work I can probably find a few extra pencils for you. _____

10. The road wound through a forest of sequoia trees. _____

11. At the snack bar she will look for some bottled water. _____

12. Mark did not remember his dental appointment. _____

 Evaluation 2: Prepositional Phrases, Personal Pronoun Usage Inside Prepositional Phrases + Verbs and Verb Phrases... ARE YOU READY?

BTW: On this evaluation there WILL be a "Prepositions Cheat Box" as well as a "Personal Pronoun Refresher Box" <u>and</u> a "Helping Verb Refresher Box."

Chapter 2

Verbs (part 2) & Subjects

One of the most important things someone can learn regarding grammar is understanding the difference between action verbs and linking verbs. Understanding many other grammar concepts will rely on your ability to tell the difference between action and linking verbs.

Most importantly, however, is that <u>action verbs make for better writing</u>, so if you can find linking verbs in your own writing, you can get rid of them!

Terms to know:

Action verb   **Subject**   **Coordinating conjunctions**
Linking verb   **Compound sentence**

2.1 – Action & Linking Verbs

A. There are two main types of verbs: Action Verbs and Linking Verbs.

B. <u>Action Verbs</u>

Sometimes the verb tells what the subject of a sentence does, did, or will be doing. This is when the verb is showing <u>action</u>. Verbs showing action are called Action Verbs.

> **Joe and Jake were playing checkers in the tent.** (The subjects, Joe and Jake, were doing something—they *were playing* checkers. So "were playing" is the verb, an action verb.)

C. <u>Linking Verbs</u>

Other times, a subject of a sentence isn't really doing anything; instead, it is just *being* something. In this case, the verb is called a Linking Verb because it <u>links</u> the subject to something it is being.

> **The waves near the reef were incredible.** (*Waves* is the subject and *incredible* is what the subject was being—these words are linked by the verb, *were*, a linking verb.)

> **The coach has been unhappy with the team's performance.** (*Coach* is the subject and *unhappy* is what the subject was being—these words are linked by this sentence's verb, "has been," a linking verb.)

How to Tell the Difference Between Linking & Action Verbs

A. There are four strategies you can use to tell if a verb is action or linking:

Strategy 1 **Use your common sense**: Is something happening in the sentence? Is the subject actually *doing* something? Is the verb you've found something you could *do*? Is the verb you've found an "action-ee" kind of word? Remember, action verbs involve mental, emotional, and physical actions.

Strategy 2 **The classics**: "Classic" linking verbs are *always* linking (when single-word verbs or as main verbs).

    a. Any form of the verb "to be": am, are, is, was, were, be, been, being
    b. Any form of the verb "to seem": seem, seems, seemed
    c. Any form of the verb "to become": become, becomes, became, becoming *

*see appendix regarding an exception—it's possible, but rare, for "to become" to be an action verb

Quick Practice

Directions: Mark the verbs in the following sentences.

    Mark action verbs with a box:

        At home I ⬚colored⬚ on the wall.

    Mark linking verbs with an "L" shape:

        The boys have been there.

    Reminder: If you find a verb phrase, be careful—do <u>not</u> include non-verbs in it!

    Example:

        After an hour the alarm was still ringing.

1. The team on the bus is leaving for a tournament in California.

2. The puzzles in that book seem easy to me.

3. On Tuesday you should try the spaghetti for lunch.

4. The horse leaped over the fence near the grandstand.

5. The weather may not become nicer over the weekend.

A closer look:

6. How many sentences above have "classic" linking verbs? _____

7. How many sentences above have verb phrases? _____

8. Which sentence above has a "polluting" word in it? _____

SCHOLAR ZONE

Most of the most basic words in English, such as personal pronouns and prepositions, come from German origin through the language of the Anglo-Saxons.

Examples of more of the thousands of Anglo-Saxon words we still use today include words like *rain, man, fear, bed, land, drink, sun, moon, house, eat,* and *milk.*

As children, English language speakers use mostly these Anglo-Saxon, or Old English, words. But English is a language influenced and enlarged by many other languages since its birth!

As we grow older, Latin words (*project, interrupt, contain*) slip into our vocabulary, as do Greek (*atlas, biology, democracy*), French (*chef, machine, café*), and more (*taco, spaghetti, cilantro, bagel, banana*)!

Whoever came up with *meow* was a genius!

©Kate Gieson &
Richbaub's Ink Works

Strategies for telling the difference between AV & LV in very difficult situations:

Strategy 3 **Replace the verb**: Replace the verb or verb phrase with a "classic" linking verb. This is a very good and popular strategy.

Example 1:

This soup tastes delicious. ➡ *is*
This soup ~~tastes~~ delicious.

If the meaning of the sentence does **not** change, then the original verb is a linking verb.

Example 2:

are
The children ~~were having~~ a great time at the party.

In this example, the meaning of the sentence changes when we replace the original verb with a known (classic) linking verb, so "were having" is an action verb.

Strategy 4 **Sentence structure**: Draw a vertical line right after the verb and look at the words to the right of your line.

In linking verb sentences, after the verb you will often find a word that describes the subject of the sentence. *In action verb sentences there will not be anything after the verb that describes the subject.*

Example:

In the afternoon the weather was becoming | really nasty. *(was becoming = LV)*

Johnny ran | three miles on the track yesterday. *(ran = AV)*

⚡ **Exercise 7**

Part 1: Surround prepositional phrases with parentheses. Verbs can never be inside prepositional phrases, so be careful. <u>One sentence does not have a prepositional phrase.</u>

1. I should have put my juice glass in the dishwasher after breakfast.

2. Before dinner we will go for a walk around the neighborhood.

3. In front of Sheila and me a long line twisted through the airport.

4. At the end of the bench that tall player looks really nervous.

5. You might enjoy the movie about the colony on Mars.

6. After college Jeremy would soon become a famous physicist.

7. That burger restaurant is the best one in the city.

8. He certainly seemed very happy to help us.

Part 2: Go back to sentences 1 - 10 above and...

mark action verbs with a box: At home I colored on the wall.

mark linking verbs with an "L" shape: The boys had never been there.

Part 3: Explain what a "verb phrase" is:

_____

_____

2.2 – Subjects

There are plenty of punctuation and usage rules that require an understanding of subjects. For instance, certain pronouns can never be used as subjects. Did you know that you can never use "me" as a subject?

In addition, as you become a more advanced writer, you will learn all about phrases and clauses, and the major difference between a phrase and a clause is that one has a subject and a verb and one doesn't.

How about this: Do you know what a compound sentence is? You should, because there is an important punctuation situation involved with compound sentences—and knowing about subjects is a key to recognizing a compound sentence.

A. A subject is the main person or thing a sentence is about. Subjects are always nouns or pronouns.

B. Most sentences have one subject, but many have two subjects. Some sentences have three or more!

Examples:

1. The test in social studies is very difficult.
Subject = *test*

2. My aunt and uncle live in New Jersey.
Subjects = *aunt, uncle* (The word *and* is not part of the subject—it's one of those connecting words called <u>conjunctions</u>.)

3. Around the corner two thieves are robbing a bank!
Subject = *thieves*

4. My ankles, feet, and toes were sore after ballet practice.
Subjects = *ankles, feet, toes*

Can you pick out the <u>verbs</u> in the sentences above?	Can you tell if they are action or linking verbs? (Circle one.)
1. _____	AV LV
2. _____	AV LV
3. _____	AV LV
4. _____	AV LV

The Relationship Between Subjects & Verbs

A. To find a verb's <u>subject</u>, first locate the verb, then ask, "Who or what _____?"

(insert verb)

Examples:

1. At the picnic on Saturday everyone loved the fried chicken.

"Who or what _loved_?" Answer = _everyone_, so _everyone_ is the subject

2. My grandmother sat near the window in her room.

"Who or what _sat_?" Answer = _grandmother_, so _grandmother_ is the subject

3. The brother and sister had similar smiles.

"Who or what _had_?" Answer = _brother, sister_

4. The construction workers are at the corner of my block.

"Who or what _are_?" Answer = _workers_

C. Notice that the subject in #4 above is NOT "construction workers." How come?

Subjects are nouns and pronouns <u>only</u>—they do NOT include things that _describe_ the subject... "Construction" describes the noun "workers," so "construction" is **not** part of the subject.

D. Also, subjects are NEVER inside prepositional phrases. What's the subject in the following sentence?

At the restaurant all of the boys ordered burritos.

Write your answer here: _____   (Were you correct?)

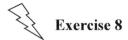 **Exercise 8**

Part 1: Surround prepositional phrases with parentheses.

1. The miniature elephant on his shelf was purchased in Kenya.

2. The woman near my dad and me wore a long blue dress.

3. At night she and I would never watch movies about scary things.

4. The lions on the savanna napped in the shade under the acacia tree.

5. Several of the stars became brighter after midnight.

Part 2: In the sentences above, mark action verbs with boxes and linking verbs with "L" shapes. Be careful of "polluted" verb phrases, and do you remember that verbs are never found inside prepositional phrases?

Part 3: Now circle the subjects in the sentences above—but be careful because, like verbs, subjects are NEVER found inside prepositional phrases.

Part 4: Below, circle the subjects in the sentences. Remember, subjects are NEVER found inside prepositional phrases.

6. Finally at the peak, the mountain climbers celebrated and took a

bunch of pictures.

7. None of my friends are going on vacation with us in April.

8. Without their star player the team still won the game.

9. For example, the girls are not allowed to wear jewelry during the

contest.

10. Does the math teacher assign homework on weekends?

 **Exercise 9**

Part 1: Surround prepositional phrases with parentheses, then mark action verbs with boxes and linking verbs with "L" shapes. Verbs can never be inside prepositional phrases so be careful.

1. The island of Zanzibar is just off the coast of Tanzania in east Africa.

2. For many years those guys were not very nice to each other.

3. In the fall we would always gather apples from the orchard.

4. Most of the sounds seemed to fade in the distance.

5. She and I will be having roasted chicken for dinner tonight.

6. The hot dogs tasted delicious with ketchup and mustard.

Part 2: In sentences 1-6, circle the subjects. Remember: Subjects are never found inside prepositional phrases.

Part 3: *Sentence Puzzles* ✚✚✚ Below, write sentences as directed. Limit your sentences to 15 words or less.

7. Begin with a prepositional phrase, and use a <u>verb phrase that is a action verb</u>:

_____

_____

8. Use a <u>single-word verb that is a linking verb</u> and two prepositional phrases:

_____

_____

about
above
across
after
against
along
around
at
before
behind
below
beneath
beside
between
beyond
by
down
during
for
from
in
in front of
inside
instead of
into
near
next to
of
off
on
out
over
through
to
toward
under
until
up
with
without

9. Use a "<u>polluted</u>" verb phrase that is an <u>linking verb</u>, and include three prepositional phrases:

_____

_____

Are you getting familiar with prepositions? I hope so since the "Prepositions Cheat Box" will soon disappear, fyi... All good things must come to an end!

Extra Practice for Evaluation 3

Part 1: Surround prepositional phrases with parentheses. Verbs can never be inside prepositional phrases so be careful. Some sentences will not have any prepositional phrases.

1. On a chilly October night in 1986 the Mets won the championship.
2. The street cleaner roared down my street yesterday.
3. Some of this recycled paper should certainly be stacked over there.
4. The pilot and copilot will make an announcement soon.
5. Under the bridge three birds had built nests on the steel girders.
6. She might become a famous actress.
7. The man in front of me and Janie was not smiling.
8. The cat and the dog snarled meanly at the mailman.
9. I saw a twister over the cornfield across the street!
10. The vanilla scented candle has been burning for three hours.

Part 2: Go back to sentences 1 - 10 above and…

Mark action verbs with a box:

At home I colored on the wall.

Mark linking verbs with an "L" shape:

The boys have been there.

Part 3: Now circle the subjects in the sentences above—but be careful because, like verbs, subjects are NEVER found inside prepositional phrases.

Part 4: Write out the four strategies you can use to tell if a verb is action or linking:

1. ____

2. ____

3. ____

4. ____

Part 5: *Sentence Puzzles* ✱✱✱ Below, write sentences as directed. Limit your sentences to 15 words or less.

11. Include two subjects, and use a verb phrase that is a linking verb:

____

____

12. Use an action verb and a prepositional phrase that has two personal pronoun o.p.'s:

____

____

13. Use a "polluted" verb phrase—action or linking—and at least two prepositional phrases.

____

____

BTW: On this evaluation there WILL be a "Prepositions Cheat Box" as well as a "Personal Pronoun Refresher Box" and a "Helping Verb Refresher Box."

Evaluation 3: Action Verbs vs. Linking Verbs + Subjects

Pun Fun

ALL YOU CAN EAT
MIDDLE EASTERN
FOOD
OPEN
©Will Gieson & Richbaub's Ink Works

"Ate too much. I falafel!"

Personal Pronouns & Subjects

A. Once more, here are the Personal Pronouns:

Objective Case Personal Pronouns	**Nominative Case Personal Pronouns**
me	I
you	you
her	she
it	it
him	he
us	we
them	they
whom	who

As you can see, *you* and *it* are all-purpose personal pronouns.

B. When using Personal Pronouns as subjects, you MUST choose a word from the Nominative Case Personal Pronouns list.

C. This is different than for prepositional phrases—in prepositional phrases you must use only Objective Case Personal Pronouns.

D. For subjects you may **only** use Nominative Case Personal Pronouns.

SCHOLAR ZONE

The Romans' language, Latin, is sometimes called a "dead" language because it is no longer widely spoken. The Latin that everyday Romans spoke evolved into other languages, including Spanish, Italian, French, Portuguese, and Romanian. Because of their roots in Roman Latin, these languages are called the "Romance" languages.

English has its early roots in Germanic languages, but over time many Latin words have crept into English, such as:

bona fide	per	versus
et cetera (etc.)	status quo	vice versa

Do you know the meanings of any of these Latin words and phrases?

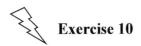 **Exercise 10**

In this exercise you will use personal pronouns.

Personal Pronoun Refresher Box

Objective Case Personal Pronouns	Nominative Case Personal Pronouns
me	I
you	you
her	she
it	it
him	he
us	we
them	they
whom	who

As you can see, *you* and *it* are all-purpose personal pronouns.

Directions: Below, fill in the blanks with <u>personal pronouns</u>. **Only use PERSONAL PRONOUNS from the box above**, but do not use "you" or "it"—that would be too easy!

1. At the mall Joe and _____ asked people for donations for the orphanage.

2. After school _____ and _____ are going to a birthday party at the park.

3. _____ and Laura waded out into the blue sea in the evening.

4. _____ and _____ have recently been trying out for the school play.

5. _____ and my dad like to fish on the beach at Huguenot State Park.

6. _____ camped near the Grand Canyon in Arizona.

7. Last summer _____ and three other families went to a concert in New York City and then did some sightseeing.

Exercise 11

Personal Pronoun Refresher Box

Objective Case Personal Pronouns	Nominative Case Personal Pronouns
me	I
you	you
her	she
it	it
him	he
us	we
them	they
whom	who

As you can see, *you* and *it* are all-purpose personal pronouns.

Part 1: Practice with using personal pronouns as <u>subjects</u>. Circle the correct personal pronouns.

1. **He/him** and **I/me** trekked at Big Boulder Park on Saturday afternoon.

2. On Tuesday **I/me** watched the spelling bee in the auditorium.

3. In the kitchen **she/her** and the butler polished the silver trays.

Part 2: Practice with personal pronouns as <u>objects of prepositions</u> (o.p.'s). Circle the correct personal pronouns.

4. Light from the candle flickered on **he/him** and **she/her**.

5. Bobby gave his extra candy to **I/me** and **she/her**.

6. Rooting for **they/them** and **we/us**, the crowd clapped loudly.

7. I walked through the mall with **she/her**.

Part 3: Putting it all together. Circle the correct personal pronouns.

8. The friends that came with **he/him** and you were really nice.

9. **We/Us** and Joey will join the soccer team in the fall.

10. While waiting for the bus, you and **she/her** might get cold.

11. (a tough one!!) **Who/Whom** did you walk to school with?

Advanced Exercise

Directions: In the sentences below, fix any personal pronouns used incorrectly. Some sentences do not have a personal pronoun error.

1. Him and Will headed for the swimming pool with Rosie and Kate.

2. The helicopter will soon land in front of he and her.

3. At the concert she and Tommy do not want to sit between you and I.

4. Jordy and him may have decided to color and to draw pictures.

5. The Devlins and us had a very nice time at the holiday picnic.

6. Who will carry the luggage for he and Doug?

7. Them and us watched the fireworks from the roof of the hotel.

8. Alex travelled with the Petersons and us to the hot springs.

9. Will you please watch the children for Mom and I?

10. For safety, stand behind us and them.

11. The dogs are trotting beside he and John.

12. This house has belonged to Mrs. Bartlett and him for 50 years.

13. Travis and they walk trails in Scotland every summer.

14. Who did Mark argue with?

15. Between Anna and me a beautiful painting hung on the wall.

Multiple Subjects, Multiple Verbs, & Compound Sentences

A. The following sentences both have two subjects and two verbs, but they are very different kinds of sentences.

    a. Jill and her sister stopped at a restaurant and ate dinner.

    b. David needed some bread, but the grocery store had already closed.

B. The main difference between the two sentences above is that in sentence "a" the verbs <u>share</u> the *same* subjects, while in sentence "b" each verb has <u>its very own subject</u>.

C. Sentence "b" is called a *compound sentence* because it is really <u>two separate sentences that</u> <u>*could* stand alone, but that have been have been joined together.</u>

D. Which of the following sentences are <u>compound</u> sentences?

    1. The water rose and washed away my sand castle.

    2. My jeans got dirty, so I put them in the laundry.

    3. Meredith has excellent grades, and she is a fabulous soccer player.

    4. In front of my house a truck lost control and skidded into a ditch.

SCHOLAR ZONE

Slowly, English evolved. That's how languages are: Words and phrases fall away, and new ones are added. "Internet" and "automobile" weren't words in Shakespeare's time! Also, you wouldn't have found the word "burrito" in an English dictionary long ago, but it's part of the English language now. And what about words like "shouldst" and "thee"? So long to them—they're hardly heard anymore.

Since there was no official dictionary during the early years of the English language—the printing press would not be invented until 1450 AD—there were all sorts of spellings and all sorts of pronunciations for many English words. With the help of the printing press, spellings began to become more consistent.

Eventually, around the year 1600, the first English language dictionary was printed and published. Finally, spellings and pronunciations would become standardized.

2.3 – Punctuating Compound Sentences

A. It's important to be able to recognize compound sentences because there's a punctuation rule for them:

> **When you join two separate sentences together to form a compound sentence, you must use either <u>a comma and a conjunction</u> OR <u>a semi-colon</u> to make the connection.**

B. Most often, a compound sentence is formed with a comma and one of the following conjunctions:

for
and
nor
but
or
yet
so

> The word *for* is a conjunction when it's being used to connect sentences. When it begins a prepositional phrase, it's a preposition.

C. These connecting words are called *coordinating conjunctions* and are often referred to by the acronym "fanboys" as their first letters spell this out.

D. Once again, connect two sentences with <u>a comma and a conjunction</u> OR <u>a semi-colon</u>:

   a. My bowl of soup was too hot**, so** I put it in the refrigerator for ten minutes.

   b. Football is a fun sport**, but** it is very rough.

   c. My sister ordered a sandwich**, and** my dad ordered a salad.

   d. Our neighbors traveled to the Grand Canyon last summer**;** my family stayed home.

E. When a sentence has more than one subject and/or more than one verb but is <u>not</u> compound, do NOT use a comma and a conjunction or a semi-colon:

   1. The skydiver jumped out of the plane and tumbled toward the earth.

   2. The snakes at the zoo frightened my mom but were totally cool to my dad and me.

   3. Thomas and his dog jumped out of the car and headed for the beach.

Exercise 12

Part 1: Write two original compound sentences. Limit each sentence to 15 words or less, and be sure to use the correct punctuation.

1. **(Use a verb phrase in this sentence.)** _____

_____

2. **(Use a linking verb in this sentence.)** _____

_____

Part 2: Insert commas or semi-colons where needed. Some sentences will not need any punctuation added. On the line after each sentence, explain why you added or did not add punctuation ("it is a compound sentence" or "it is not compound").

3. The teacher made a new seating chart and everyone was happy.

_____

4. The gardener raked up the leaves and trimmed the shrubs.

_____

5. You can have oatmeal for breakfast or you can have pancakes.

_____

6. We went on a field trip to Washington D.C. for we had studied all about the American government in social studies.

_____

7. In the cabinet I found some cereal and poured myself a bowl for breakfast.

_____

8. He and I will be on the same flight we should arrive at the meeting at the same time.

_____

 **Exercise 13**

Part 1: Surround prepositional phrases with parentheses, mark action verbs with boxes and linking verbs with "L" shapes, AND circle subjects.

1. For summer vacation you should always go to the beach.

2. My dad and I played soccer against the neighborhood kids.

3. Some of my teammates were wearing long blue socks.

4. I travelled down the road, and I saw three turtles in a pond.

5. Those burgers on the grill smell delicious.

6. The problems on page six seem too difficult for me and Mike.

Part 2: Fix personal pronouns used incorrectly.

7. The alligator slowly crawled toward my mom and I.

8. The Walkers and us arrived before Lisa and him.

9. From Portland we drove north for a scenic journey with she and my uncle.

Part 3: Insert commas or semi-colons if needed.

10. Around eight o'clock we went outside on the porch and my mom made us a cup of hot chocolate.

11. He and Sally joined the team and quickly became our best players.

12. For lunch we had grilled cheese sandwiches we didn't have time for dessert.

| about |
| above |
| across |
| after |
| against |
| along |
| around |
| at |
| before |
| behind |
| below |
| beneath |
| beside |
| between |
| beyond |
| by |
| down |
| during |
| for |
| from |
| in |
| in front of |
| inside |
| instead of |
| into |
| near |
| next to |
| of |
| off |
| on |
| out |
| over |
| through |
| to |
| toward |
| under |
| until |
| up |
| with |
| without |

Part 1: Circle the correct personal pronouns.

1. We and **they/them** are meeting for dinner near the beach.

2. James did his homework with Tara and **she/her**.

3. **He/him** and Donnie picked tulips in Holland over the summer.

4. Next to the couch Mike and **she/her** played backgammon for two hours.

5. Sand from the dunes blew on Jane and **I/me**.

6. Between Kate and **he/him** I could see my lost book.

Part 2: Insert commas or semi-colons where needed. Some sentences will not need any punctuation added.

7. After school I went to my friend's house and we played basketball in his driveway.

8. The story got really exciting in chapter 13 I couldn't put the book down!

9. On Saturday morning my mom told me to do my homework and to make my bed.

10. We forgot to pick up Joe so his mom called to complain.

Part 3: *Sentence Puzzles* ✦✦✦ Below, write sentences as directed. Limit your sentences to 15 words or less.

11. Write an original compound sentence that includes a verb phrase. <u>Be sure to use the correct punctuation.</u>

_____

_____

12. Write an original sentence that has two subjects and one verb where BOTH subjects are personal pronouns.

_____

_____

Part 4: Surround prepositional phrases with parentheses, mark action verbs with boxes and linking verbs with "L" shapes, AND circle subjects.

13. The deer looked nervous, and it quickly darted away from us.

14. Her glasses were found at the checkout counter in the library.

15. Under an orange sunset the waves rolled up onto the beach and wet our feet.

16. For dinner a few of us will be having pizza; the others will have subs.

17. Some riders became lost in the woods during the hunt.

18. From the back seat I could see lots of traffic ahead.

19. She and they did not agree with us about the movie.

20. We never received the package, but we did receive your letter.

BTW: On this evaluation there WILL be a "Prepositions Cheat Box" and a "Personal Pronoun Refresher Box"

 Evaluation 4: Pronoun Usage with Prepositional Phrases and Subjects, Punctuating Compound Sentences, and Linking Verbs vs. Action Verbs

Chapter 3

Comma Review

3.1 – Comma Usage with Introductory Prepositional Phrases

A. **After one introductory prepositional phrase** (a prepositional phrase at the very beginning of a sentence), **you should mostly <u>avoid</u> using a comma:**

Compare the following sentences:

> At school I look forward to recess the most.

> At school, I look forward to recess the most.

The comma in the second sentence above is <u>not</u> necessary and should therefore be omitted.

B. **Once in a while, you need to use a comma after a single introductory prepositional phrase in order to avoid confusion.**

Compare the following sentences:

> To some French dressing on a salad adds zest to any meal.

> To some, French dressing on a salad adds zest to any meal.

The comma definitely helps—without the pause you might think the sentence is about either how only some *French* people like dressing on their salads or even how some French folks enjoy getting *dressed* on top of a salad!

C. **After phrases like "for example," "in other words," "in conclusion," "by the way," etc., it's ok to use a comma.**

D. After <u>more than one</u> introductory prepositional phrase, commas are more acceptable but still optional:

Compare the following sentences:

In the corner of my bedroom I saw a large spider climbing the wall.

In the corner of my bedroom, I saw a large spider climbing the wall.

The comma in the second sentence is acceptable since there are two prepositional phrases beginning the sentence, but is it really necessary?

E. The bottom line? All good writers know that you should avoid unnecessary commas, so **after prepositional phrases at the beginning of sentences, if you can do without a comma, don't use one!**

<u>Quick Practice</u>: Add a comma only where absolutely needed in the following sentences.

1. In the cabinet under the sink you can find a new bar of soap.

2. With spaghetti I like to have a little meat sauce.

3. On Saturday mornings are usually spent doing chores around the house.

4. At the dance on Friday we ate pizza and talked more than we danced.

5. By the way did you notice that Mr. Leonard wore a new tie today?

3.2 – Commas in Dialogue

A. Look at the <u>commas</u> in the following exchange between Laura and Jenny:

1. "You told me I could buy this candy bar for one dollar," said Laura.

2. Jenny replied, "That's not what I said."

3. "Oh, sorry," said Laura.

4. Jenny said, "You can have it for free!"

B. Always use a comma when introducing a quotation with something like "Bob said" or "Joe asked," etc., as in lines two and four above.

C. At the end of a quotation, if you're going to say who said it, put a <u>comma</u> at the end of the quotation, such as in lines one and three above.

Of course, if the quotation is something that's exclaimed or if the quotation is a question, the end-of-quotation punctuation would be an exclamation point or a question mark instead of a comma.

Quick Practice: Add commas and end marks to the following dialogue:

Max said " Do you like peanut butter "

" No, I don't like peanut butter " answered Ann

" Then I guess we can't be friends " said Max

Surprised, Ann said " Wow. You must really love peanut butter "

Did you notice that end-of-quotation punctuation always goes <u>inside</u> the end quotation mark?

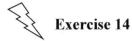 **Exercise 14**

Part 1: Add commas where necessary. Some sentences will not need a comma. No sentence will need more than one comma.

1. After the speech Mary stood up and said "I would like to volunteer."

2. For example the temperature in March never goes below 70 degrees.

3. "In baseball most fastballs travel at 90 miles per hour " explained Eli.

4. Before takeoff I put my seatbelt on and flipped through a magazine.

5. "Please put your pencils down. The quiz is over " said the professor.

6. After lunch time really seems to slow down at school.

7. On Tuesday I have an appointment with my dentist.

Part 2: Add commas to the following dialogue.

1   The wedding had been splendid, and now the newly married

2   couple was off on their honeymoon in Paris.

3   "I can't wait to see our hotel " said Mabry.

4   "Me either " replied Tommy, Mabry's new husband.

5   "Are we in the right part of town?" said Mabry. "This doesn't

6   look quite right. Shouldn't we be able to see the Eiffel Tower by now?"

7   The taxi driver heard Mabry's question and said "It is ok, Madam.

8   In ten minutes we will be there." Forty minutes later, it was beginning

9   to look hopeless; they were driving through wheat fields. Finally, the

10 driver admitted "I am lost. I am sorry, sir."

11   "Ugh " said Tommy.

Did you notice how paragraphs change when speakers change?

3.3 – Punctuating Compound Sentences

A. As discussed in Chapter 2, when you join two separate sentences together to form a compound sentence, you must use either <u>a comma and a conjunction</u> OR <u>a semi-colon</u> to make the connection.

     b. My sister ordered a sandwich**,** **and** my dad ordered a salad.

     d. Our neighbors traveled to Disney World**;** my family stayed home.

B. When a sentence has more than one subject and/or more than one verb but is <u>not</u> compound, do NOT use a comma and a conjunction or a semi-colon:

     1. The skydiver jumped out of the plane and tumbled toward the earth.

     2. The snakes at the zoo frightened my mom and gave me nightmares!

Quick Practice: Add a comma or a semi colon where necessary in the following sentences.

1. The birds came to the feeder each morning and we watched them from our kitchen window.

2. The goalie was ready but the opponent didn't take any shots.

3. I found the switch and turned the lights on.

4. High up on the mountain the winds blew furiously so the ski lift had to be shut down.

5. My team has trouble scoring points it's going to be a long season.

6. We spread tomato sauce and sprinkled mozzarella cheese on the bread and put it in the oven for 15 minutes.

3.4 – Comma Usage with Introductory Participial Phrases

A. Do you recall what a participial phrase is? The sentences below all begin with one:

1. <u>Running like mad from the defender</u>, the quarterback threw a desperate pass to his favorite receiver.

2. <u>Slowed by the heavy traffic</u>, Mark would arrive late to his grandma's house.

3. <u>Talking quickly</u>, my mom told the nurse about my accident.

Did you notice the commas that <u>follow</u> each participial phrase above? Yes, those commas are NECESSARY. Don't forget the comma when you begin a sentence with a participial phrase.

B. A **participial phrase** is a phrase (a group of words without a subject-verb pair) that begins with an *–ing* or *–ed* verb.* Participial phrases are **descriptive** (adjective) phrases.

1. <u>Cooked perfectly</u>, the chicken fillets were tender and juicy.
2. <u>Watching his teacher grab a huge stack of stapled packets</u>, Alex became very nervous about the math test.
3. <u>Concentrating on the toy mouse</u>, the kitten suddenly sprang and attacked!

Did you notice that the participial phrases above all describe the sentence's subject, which immediately follows the participial phrase?

C. It's possible to begin a sentence with an *–ing* phrase that is NOT a participial phrase:

Jogging in the park is great exercise.

Above, "jogging in the park" is not describing anything. This is a noun phrase that we call a *gerund phrase*, and there is no comma required in this sentence. Be careful: Do not confuse participial and gerund phrases. Remember, participial phrases are ***descriptive*** phrases.

*Some verbs in the past tense do not have an –ed form. See appendix.

Quick Practice: Add commas where necessary in each sentence. Some sentences may not need a comma added.

1. Toasted to a crispy brown the marshmallow was headed for my mouth!

2. Driving way too fast Teddy was scaring all of the passengers in his car.

3. In my backyard we played kickball until dark.

4. Walking down the street I saw a squirrel collecting acorns for the winter.

SCHOLAR ZONE

Modern English is what Shakespeare used to write his plays between approximately 1590 and 1613... But everyone knows Shakespeare is tough to understand! Early "Modern" English is not super easy for most present-day English speakers to understand.

Here's a chunk of text from Shakespeare's *Romeo and Juliet* describing Romeo. Can you understand it?

...Verona brags of him
To be a virtuous and well-governed youth.
I would not for the wealth of all the town
Here in my house do him disparagement.
Therefore be patient. Take no note of him.

Slowly, slowly, slowly, the language changes... Here's how the above passage might be written today:

He has a great reputation in Verona.
He is a good and well-behaved young man.
I would never, even if you paid me,
Insult him here in my house.
Relax. Ignore him.

But the evolution and flexibility of English is so cool. Can you imagine a super modern version of the Shakespeare passage above? If so, write it below!

_____

_____

_____

_____

_____

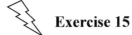 **Exercise 15**

Directions: Add commas or semi colons where necessary. Some sentences will not need a comma or a semi colon. **No sentence will need more than one comma or semi colon.**

1. In the red room two couches face each other and a large bookcase stands in the corner.

2. Thinking that he might get chilly he grabbed a sweatshirt from his drawer.

3. Worried about the predicted frost we covered the budding roses with a blanket overnight.

4. Over those hills near the reservoir there are some great biking trails.

5. "Henri Matisse is my favorite artist " said my uncle.

6. Fishing the flats in the Caribbean for bonefish looks fun one day I am going to do that!

7. At a restaurant meals often contain way more calories than meals prepared at home.

8. On Tuesday we are going to visit the museum downtown.

9. At rush hour the highways are filled with cars and trucks heading home after a long workday.

10. After our hike we pitched our tents and collected sticks for the fire.

11. "Don't forget to pack the sunscreen " said my mom.

12. His pencil broke before the test so I gave him one of mine to use.

3.5 – The Appositive Phrase (very ubiquitous)

(*ubiquitous* = found everywhere)

A. An appositive phrase is a small, unnecessary descriptive phrase that comes right after a noun. Appositives can be another noun or a noun with a descriptive word or two. An appositive phrase may also include a prepositional phrase:

1. My son, <u>a surfer</u>, is six feet tall.

2. My friend accidentally crashed into the p.e. teacher, <u>a tall bearded man</u>, during our dodge ball game.

3. Yesterday, his boss, <u>Mary</u>, asked him if he could work over the weekend.

4. The train sped through Chester, <u>a small town near the sea</u>.

Did you notice the commas that surround each appositive phrase above? Yes, those commas are NECESSARY. Don't forget the commas when you use appositive phrases.

B. **Please note that appositive phrases do NOT include verbs.**

<u>Quick Practice #2:</u> Below, try creating appositive phrases to describe the nouns that come just before the blank lines.

1. My school, _____ , is on East Roosevelt Street.

2. My brother gave Paul, _____ , his old guitar.

⚡ **Exercise 16**

Part 1: On the line, name the underlined phrase (prepositional, participial, or appositive).

_____ 1. Orion, <u>a famous constellation,</u> is named after a hunter in Greek

mythology.

_____ 2. <u>Generating massive amounts of hydroelectric power,</u> the Hoover

Dam was built in the 1930's.

_____ 3. The magazines <u>under the table</u> are mainly travel magazines.

_____ 4. My house, <u>a bungalow,</u> was built in 1963.

_____ 5. <u>Exhausted from a long day babysitting his cousins,</u> Cobie went to

bed immediately after dinner.

Part 2: Add commas or semi colons where necessary. Some sentences will not need a comma or a semi colon.

1. My best friend has a German shepherd and I have a St. Bernard.

2. Catching a pop up to end the inning Hillary jogged off the field and into the dugout.

3. The brass section of the seventh grade band was excellent they must have practiced hard!

4. I drink tea in my favorite mug a ceramic New York Mets mug every morning before work.

5. I pulled my dress shoes from the closet before the dance and shined them with shoe polish.

6. Designed by Frank Lloyd Wright the house on the corner of my street is for sale.

7. I was surprised when Mom said "Would you like another chocolate bar?"

Chapter 4

Description 101: Adjectives & Adverbs

4.1 – Adjectives

Understanding adjectives goes WAY beyond knowing about the words that describe nouns and pronouns!

First of all, there's a certain type of adjective which you've probably never heard of: the <u>predicate adjective</u>. You'll be learning about predicate adjectives and their close cousins, <u>predicate nominatives</u>. Understanding these descriptive words will add to your knowledge about when to use "me" vs. when to use "I" (and all of the other personal pronouns).

Secondly, as you become a more advanced writer, you will discover giant groups of words—phrases and clauses— that also function as adjectives. Knowing about <u>adjective phrases and clauses</u> will add a whole new sophistication to your sentence structures, and it will help you understand some important punctuation rules. This chapter will help to prepare you for those future lessons.

A. Adjectives are words that describe nouns and pronouns, which is the same thing as saying that adjectives describe people, places, things, and ideas.

B. Adjectives are easy to use and easy to spot. Can you find the adjective in the following sentence?

She snuck through the halls in red sneakers.

C. Of course "red" pops out as describing the noun *sneakers*. Aren't adjectives easy?

©Richbaub's Ink Works

Exercise 17

Part 1: Write adjective-noun pairs—come up with a noun and put an adjective before it:

1. _____

2. _____

3. _____

4. _____

5. _____

Part 2: Write prepositional phrases that have adjectives describing the o.p.'s (objects of the preposition).

6. _____

7. _____

8. _____

about
above
across
after
against
along
around
at
before
behind
below
beneath
beside
between
beyond
by
down
during
for
from
in
in front of
inside
instead of
into
near
next to
of
off
on
out
over
through
to
toward
under
until
up
with
without

Quick Fact: The most common adjectives in the world are the "Articles." The Articles are *a*, *an*, and *the*.

Here's a sentence that, technically, includes <u>three</u> adjectives:

The chef cut an orange with a knife.

<u>For our purposes, though, when hunting for Adjectives, we will ignore Articles—there are just too many of them!!</u>

The Locations of Adjectives

A. Most adjectives are found just before a noun—like in the adjective-noun pairs in the previous exercise. Here's another example:

The warm sunshine spread across the lawn.

Above, *warm* is an adjective describing the noun *sunshine*.

B. However, adjectives can also be found <u>reaching back over linking verbs to describe the subject</u> of a sentence. Here are some examples:

1. Everyone was cold.

Above, *cold* is an adjective describing *everyone*, the subject of the sentence.

2. The children on the swings seemed happy.

Above, *happy* is an adjective describing the subject *children*.

C. Adjectives after linking verbs—the adjectives that reach back to describe subjects—are called **Predicate Adjectives.** *

1. "Regular" Adjective: The <u>tall</u> building rose into the clouds.

2. Predicate Adjective: Your grade on the test was <u>excellent</u>! **

* see appendix regarding other terms used for predicate adjectives

** see appendix about a tricky situation that may arise with verb phrases and predicate adjectives

Exercise 18

Part 1: Write prepositional phrases that have regular adjectives describing the o.p.'s (objects of the preposition).

1. _____

2. _____

3. _____

In Part 2 you'll need to use linking verbs:

"Classic" Linking Verb Refresher Box

Any form of the verb "to be": **am, are, is, was, were, be, been, being**
Any form of the verb "to seem": **seem, seems, seemed**
Any form of the verb "to become": **become, becomes, became, becoming**

Part 2: *Sentence Puzzles* ✲✲✲ Carefully follow the directions for each sentence, and **be sure** to use a DIFFERENT VERB in each sentence.

4. Write a sentence that has a prepositional phrase and a Predicate Adjective. (Remember, in order to have a Predicate Adjective your verb phrase must be a linking verb.)

_____

_____

5. Write a sentence that has a <u>pronoun</u> for a subject, a Predicate Adjective, and two prepositional phrases. (Remember, in order to have a Predicate Adjective your verb must be a linking verb.)

_____

_____

6. Write a sentence that has two <u>personal pronouns</u> for subjects, one verb, and a Predicate Adjective. (Remember, in order to have a Predicate Adjective your verb must be a linking verb.)

_____

_____

7. Write a sentence that includes two regular adjectives, begins with a prepositional phrase, and <u>has a "polluted" verb phrase</u>.

_____

_____

about
above
across
after
against
along
around
at
before
behind
below
beneath
beside
between
beyond
by
down
during
for
from
in
in front of
inside
instead of
into
near
next to
of
off
on
out
over
through
to
toward
under
until
up
with
without

 **Extra Practice with Adjectives**

Directions: Draw a single underline beneath regular <u>adjectives</u> and a double underline beneath <u>predicate adjectives</u> in the following sentences. **Each sentence has exactly <u>two</u> adjectives.**

**Be sure to mark prepositional phrases, verbs, and subjects BEFORE you make your final decisions about adjectives!

1. The lighted bridge over the river looks magnificent at night.

2. The winning catch in the championship game was made by Thomas.

3. On Monday my mom may still take me to the new mall.

4. By the way, Susan and I do not enjoy long, scary movies.

5. The crossing guard near school seems really unfriendly.

6. David and he should arrive at the downtown airport with three suitcases.

7. This soup tastes delicious!

8. Cheesy broccoli is yummy!

9. Between David and him sat a tiny gray mouse.

10. Could you lend me your eraser for the math test?

4.2 – Predicate Adjectives vs. Predicate Nominatives

A. Predicate Adjectives have a close cousin called *Predicate Nominatives*.

B. A Predicate Nominative, like a Predicate Adjective, is found after a linking verb and it reaches back over the verb to describe the subject.

C. However, Predicate Nominatives are not actually adjectives; they are nouns and pronouns.

D. Take a look at some examples—the underlined words are Predicate <u>Nominatives</u>:

My father was a <u>fireman</u>.

The centerpiece at the wedding will be a carved ice <u>statue</u>.

He becomes an absolute <u>maniac</u> on the football field.

Have you ever been an <u>actor</u> in a play?

E. In each sentence above, the underlined words reach back over linking verbs to describe the subjects. Also, each descriptive word is actually a <u>noun</u>, so they are called Predicate *Nominatives* instead of Predicate *Adjectives*.

F. Here are some more examples of the similarities and differences between Predicate Adjectives and Predicate Nominatives:

> **This coffee is hot.** (*Hot* describes the subject *coffee*, and since the word *hot* is an adjective, it is a Predicate <u>Adjective</u>.)

> **After six weeks the larvae became a butterfly.** (*Butterfly* describes the subject *larvae*, and since the word *butterfly* is a noun, it is a Predicate <u>Nominative</u>.)

G. Keep in mind that not all linking verb sentences have Predicate Adjectives and Predicate Nominatives:

> **I have never been on a roller coaster.**

> **The girls were at their lockers before class.**

A Trick for Finding Predicate Adjectives & Predicate Nominatives

A. If you're looking at a sentence that has a linking verb and you're wondering how to locate the Predicate Adjective or Predicate Nominative, there is a little trick you can use.

B. Make a little question using this formula: "S + V + who or what?"

Example:

The children became cold at the ballgame.

Take your subject *children* and your verb *became* and ask "who or what?"

"Children became <u>who or what?</u>"

C. The answer, *cold*, is your Predicate Adjective or Predicate Nominative—now decide if you've found a descriptive word or a person, place, thing, or idea.

D. A descriptive word would be a Predicate Adjective, while a person, place, thing or idea would be a Predicate Nominative.

E. In the example, *cold* is a descriptive word, so it's a Predicate <u>Adjective</u>.

F. Please note: Predicate Nominatives are NEVER found inside prepositional phrases!

©Richbaub's Ink Works

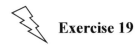 **Exercise 19**

You'll need to use linking verbs in this exercise:

"Classic" Linking Verb Refresher Box
Any form of the verb "to be": **am, are, is, was, were, be, been, being**
Any form of the verb "to seem": **seem, seems, seemed**
Any form of the verb "to become": **become, becomes, became, becoming**

Part 1: Write sentences that have Predicate Nominatives. Remember, only <u>linking verb</u> sentences have Predicate Nominatives. Limit your sentences to 12 words or less and **use a DIFFERENT VERB for each sentence**.

1. _____

2. **(Use a verb phrase in this sentence.)** _____

_____

Part 2: Write sentences that have Predicate Adjectives. Remember, only <u>linking verb</u> sentences have Predicate Adjectives. Limit your sentences to 12 words or less and **use a DIFFERENT VERB for each sentence**.

3. _____

4. **(Use a "polluted" verb phrase in this sentence.)** _____

_____

Part 3: In the following linking verb sentences, find and label Predicate Adjectives (PA) and Predicate Nominatives (PN).

5. According to the weatherman, seas will become dangerous later today.

6. The social studies teacher seems quite nice.

7. That party was a little too crazy for me!

8. My opponent is a great warrior.

Part 3: Write prepositional phrases that have regular adjectives describing the o.p.'s (objects of the prepositions).

9. _____

10. _____

Extra Practice for Evaluation 5

Part 1:

1. In your own words, explain the difference between a "regular" adjective and a Predicate Adjective:

_____

_____

2. Below, circle ALL adjectives.

He was sleepy.   at the piano concert   the blind man

3. Above, which circled word is a Predicate Adjective? _____

4. In your own words, explain the difference between a Predicate Adjective and a Predicate Nominative:

_____

_____

Part 2: Over each underlined word, write ADJ (regular adjective), PA (Predicate Adjective), or PN (Predicate Nominative).

5. Kristina wore red flats, and Sonya's high heels were <u>black</u>.

6. The sea warmed in the <u>afternoon</u> sun.

7. My dad and I sailed on a <u>magnificent</u> yacht from Boston to Nantucket.

8. That math test was a <u>nightmare</u>!

Part 3: In the following linking verb sentences, find and label Predicate Adjectives (PA) and Predicate Nominatives (PN).

9. The horse Secretariat was the Triple Crown Champion in 1973.

10. Your brother's behavior seems a bit odd to me.

11. I will become a doctor one day.

Part 4: *Sentence Puzzles* ✜✛✜ Carefully follow the directions for each sentence.

12. Write a sentence with two personal pronouns for subjects and just one **regular** adjective.

_____

13. Write a brand new, original sentence using the linking verb "will be" that also has a Predicate Nominative.

_____

14. Write a brand new, original sentence using the linking verb *seems* that also has a Predicate Adjective.

_____

 Evaluation 5: **Introduction to Adjectives, including Predicate Adjectives and Predicate Nominatives**

Pun Fun

4.3 – Predicate Nominatives & Personal Pronouns

A. Guess what? Remember those annoying little Personal Pronouns? Well, they're back!

B. When you use a personal pronoun as a Predicate Nominative, you must choose a <u>Nominative Case</u> Personal Pronoun.

Once again, here are all of the Personal Pronouns:

Objective Case Personal Pronouns	**Nominative Case Personal Pronouns**
me	I
you	you
her	she
it	it
him	he
us	we
them	they
whom	who

As you can see, *you* and *it* are both objective <u>and</u> nominative case personal pronouns.

> Use for Predicate Nominatives …Get it? *Nominative* Case for Predicate *Nominatives.* Pretty clever, huh?

C. Here are some examples:

I admitted that the thief was <u>I</u>.

For the school play the directors will be <u>she and I</u>. (Two predicate nominatives)

D. Something worth noting here is that our rule for personal pronouns and prepositional phrases hasn't changed! You still must use <u>Objective Case</u> Personal Pronouns inside prepositional phrases:

Those presents are (for <u>me</u>.)

They were (with <u>us</u>) yesterday.

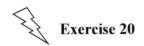 **Exercise 20**

You'll need to use linking verbs in this exercise.

"Classic" Linking Verb Refresher Box

Any form of the verb "to be": **am, are, is, was, were, be, been, being**
Any form of the verb "to seem": **seem, seems, seemed**
Any form of the verb "to become": **become, becomes, became, becoming**

You will also need to use personal pronouns in this exercise.

Personal Pronoun Refresher Box

Objective Case Personal Pronouns	Nominative Case Personal Pronouns
me	I
you	you
her	she
it	it
him	he
us	we
them	they
whom	who

As you can see, *you* and *it* are both objective <u>and</u> nominative case personal pronouns.

Part 1: *Sentence Puzzles* ✦✦✦ Write sentences as directed.

1. Write a sentence that has a personal pronoun for a Predicate Nominative. Remember to use a <u>linking</u> verb and a <u>nominative case</u> personal pronoun. Limit your sentence to 12 words or less.

_____

_____

2. Write a sentence that has a Predicate Adjective. Remember to use a <u>linking</u> verb. Limit your sentence to 12 words or less. **(Do NOT use the same verb you used in the sentence above!)**

_____

_____

3. Write a sentence that has <u>two</u> Predicate Nominatives where both are personal pronouns. Remember to use a <u>linking</u> verb and <u>nominative case</u> personal pronouns. Limit your sentence to 12 words or less. **(Do NOT repeat any of the verbs used in the sentences above!)**

_____

_____

Part 2: In the following sentences, surround the prepositional phrases with parentheses. (Ignore the blank lines after each sentence for now—you will use them in Part 7.)

4. The hungry dog grabbed a sandwich from the table. _____

5. During the test Matt seemed confused. _____

6. On the green hill over yonder the cows munched on grass.

_____

Part 3: Mark the verbs. Use a box for action verbs and an "L" shape for linking verbs.

Part 4: Circle the subjects.

Part 5: Each sentence has either one adjective OR one Predicate Adjective—underline it.

Part 6: Draw an arrow from the adjective or Predicate Adjective to the word being described.

Part 7: Finally, after each sentence identify the word being described (by the adjective or Predicate Adjective) as a Subject (S) or Object of the Preposition (OP).

about
above
across
after
against
along
around
at
before
behind
below
beneath
beside
between
beyond
by
down
during
for
from
in
in front of
inside
instead of
into
near
next to
of
off
on
out
over
through
to
toward
under
until
up
with
without

Extra Practice for Evaluation 6

Part 1: In the blank after each sentence, identify the underlined word as either an adjective (ADJ), Predicate Adjective (PA), or Predicate Nominative (PN).

1. She should have been more <u>careful</u> with her money. _____

2. Rover's barking was a great burglar <u>alarm</u>. _____

3. Her statements about the suspect were completely <u>true</u>. _____

4. The car in my uncle's garage is a 1969 <u>Mustang</u>. _____

5. My mom and I looked exhausted after our <u>shopping</u> trip. _____

Part 2:   *Sentence Puzzles* �   Write sentences as directed.

6. Write a sentence that has a Predicate Adjective. Remember to use a <u>linking</u> verb. Limit your sentence to 12 words or less.

_____

_____

7. Write a sentence that has <u>two personal pronoun Predicate Nominatives</u>. Don't forget to use a <u>linking</u> verb. Limit your sentence to 12 words or less.

_____

_____

8. Write a sentence that has an <u>action</u> verb, <u>three</u> regular adjectives, and a <u>verb phrase</u>.

_____

_____

Part 3: Write prepositional phrases that have adjectives describing the o.p.'s (objects of the preposition).

9. _____   11. _____

10. _____   12. _____

BTW: There will be "Personal Pronoun Refresher Box" and a "Classic Linking Verb Refresher Box" on the test.

Evaluation 6: Adjectives, Including Predicate Adjectives, + Pronoun Usage with Predicate Nominatives

4.4 – Adverbs

Adverbs are the evil cousins of adjectives, for although their purpose, like adjectives, is to describe, exactly how or what an adverb describes is not always clear to students.

Once you get it, though, your knowledge of adverbs comes in handy when trying to write and speak well. For instance, deciding when to use "well" vs. when to use "good" has to do with knowing about adverbs. In addition, a popular technique you can use to improve your sentence variety is to begin sentences with adverbs once in a while.

Later, when you become a more advanced writer, you will discover groups of words—phrases and clauses—that also function as adverbs, and certain punctuation and sentence variety concepts are connected to a knowledge of these things...

A. Adverbs are the most difficult part of speech. Like adjectives, adverbs are descriptive words, but, unlike adjectives, <u>adverbs do **not** describe nouns and pronouns</u>.

B. Adverbs describe verbs, adjectives, as well as other adverbs.

C. Adjectives and adverbs at work:

ADJECTIVES AT WORK	ADVERBS AT WORK
<u>giant</u> ocean	<u>incredibly</u> famous
<u>blue</u> fabric	walk <u>quickly</u>
<u>famous</u> actor	<u>very</u> quietly

The Questions Adverbs Answer

A. The most important thing to know about adverbs is that whenever they describe something, they answer one of the following questions about whatever it is they're describing:

"When?"   "Where?"   "How?"

B. Practice examples:

1.) **Yesterday we rode our bikes to the park.**

THE ADVERB *yesterday* ANSWERS (circle one)
   A. *when?*
   B. *where?*
   C. *how?*

ABOUT THE WORD *rode*, WHICH IS A(N) (circle one)
   A. *verb*
   B. *adjective*
   C. *adverb*

2.) **The Pearsons will be building a house here in the fall.**

THE ADVERB *here* ANSWERS (circle one)
   A. *when?*
   B. *where?*
   C. *how?*

ABOUT *will be building*, WHICH IS A(N) (circle one)
   A. *verb*
   B. *adjective*
   C. *adverb*

Are you getting the hang of adverbs?

C. More practice examples:

1.) David gently rocked the baby.

THE ADVERB *gently* ANSWERS (circle one) *when? where? how?*

ABOUT *rocked* , WHICH IS A(N) (circle one) *verb   adjective   adverb*

2.) They will be arriving very soon.

(There are <u>two</u> adverbs in sentence "2.")

THE ADVERB *soon* ANSWERS (circle one) *when? where? how?*

ABOUT *will be arriving*, WHICH IS A(N) (circle one) *verb   adjective   adverb*

IN ADDITION, THE ADVERB *very* ANSWERS (circle one) *when? where? how?*

ABOUT *soon*, WHICH IS A(N) (circle one) *verb   adjective   adverb*

Pun
Fun

Sir Lancelot with his lesser-known
brother, Sir Render.

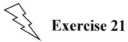 **Exercise 21**

Part 1: Fill in the blank with an adverb that answers the question below the blank.

1. we will eat _____
                        (When?)

2. ran _____ around the track
          (How?)

3. were _____ studying for a big test
            (When?)

4. _____ turned left
          (How?)

5. sat _____
          (Where?)

6. _____ bright jacket
          (How?)

Part 2: Locating adjectives

> **Here's a terrific way to look at the difference between adjectives and adverbs:**
>
> **Adjectives** describe nouns and pronouns (people, places, things, and ideas)
>
> **Adverbs** answer When? Where? and How?

In items 1 through 6 above, there are two adjectives (ignore the articles). Write the adjectives below:

7. _____

8. _____

The Hunt for Adverbs

A. What's most difficult about adverbs is that an adverb's location in a sentence doesn't follow any kind of pattern.

B. For instance, so far we've seen that nouns and pronouns can be **subjects**, **objects of prepositions**, and **predicate nominatives** (PN's). Each of these things is found in certain areas of a sentence:

- subjects toward the beginning
- o.p.'s at the end of prepositional phrases
- and predicate nominatives after linking verbs

C. So when you're looking for nouns and pronouns, you have an idea of where they can be found.

D. The locations of verbs, adjectives, and Predicate Adjectives (PA's) are also pretty consistent.

- Verbs are predictably found toward the middle of a sentence
- Adjectives are typically right next to the words they describe
- Predicate Adjectives are always after linking verbs

E. Adverbs aren't so predictable. Below, look again at the sentences we were working with. **The adverbs are all over the place!**

> **<u>Yesterday</u> we rode our bikes to the park.**
>
> **The Pearsons will be building a house <u>here</u> in the fall.**
>
> **David <u>gently</u> rocked the baby.**
>
> **They will be arriving <u>very</u> <u>soon</u>.**

F. However, if you have a set routine for analyzing sentences, you'll be in good shape!

Getting into "The Routine"

A. So far, we've emphasized the following routine:

> **First,** surround prepositional phrases with parentheses.
> **Second,** mark the verb(s) with a box (action verb) or an "L" shape (linking verb).
> **Third,** circle the subject(s).

On any kind of grammar exercise, you should ALWAYS approach each sentence this way; it will help immensely in your hunt for <u>adjectives</u> and <u>adverbs</u>.

B. Only <u>after</u> completing "The Routine" should you look for your descriptive words, <u>adjectives</u> and <u>adverbs</u>.

C. Let's begin the hunt for adjectives and adverbs by running through an example:

(After the meal) the (children) sat quietly (in the family room.)

D. Above, the descriptive words should stand out because you have eliminated some words from consideration:

- Your subject is not an adjective or adverb (subjects are always nouns or pronouns).

- Your verb is obviously not an adjective or adverb!

- In the prepositional phrases, you know that the first word is a preposition and the last word (o.p.) is a noun or pronoun.

- You should also remember that between the preposition and the o.p. there can be descriptive words, so that's a good place to look for adjectives and adverbs.

E. In our example sentence…

> *quietly* is an **adverb** answering the question "how?" about the verb *sat*

> *family* is an **adjective** describing the noun *room*

F. Here are some more examples. Be sure to follow "**The Routine**" <u>before</u> looking for adjectives (regular adjectives, not PA's) and adverbs!

1. The fiery coach became extremely upset with his players.

    First, surround prepositional phrases with parentheses.
    Second, mark the verb(s) with a box (action verb) or an "L" shape (linking verb).
    Third, circle the subject(s).

Adverb: _____

(regular) Adjectives: _____ & _____

This sentence also has a Predicate Adjective (PA): _____

2. Tomorrow your substitute teacher will be Mrs. Page.

    First, surround prepositional phrases with parentheses.
    Second, mark the verb(s) with a box (action verb) or an "L" shape (linking verb).
    Third, circle the subject(s).

Adverb: _____

(regular) Adjectives: _____ & _____

3. I have never asked my teacher for extra help.

    First, surround prepositional phrases with parentheses.
    Second, mark the verb(s) with a box (action verb) or an "L" shape (linking verb).
    Third, circle the subject(s).

Adverb: _____

Adjectives: _____ & _____

 Yep, those "polluting" words are ALWAYS adverbs!

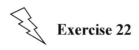 **Exercise 22**

Use "The Routine":

> **First,** surround prepositional phrases with parentheses.
> **Second,** mark the verb(s) with a box (action verb) or an "L" shape (linking verb).
> **Third,** circle the subject(s).
> **Then and only then,** identify adjectives and adverbs.

1. The boy in the red car is walking slowly toward the school.

   Adjective(s):

   Adverb(s):

2. Under the porch you can barely see seven little kittens.

   Adjective(s):

   Adverb(s):

3. On sunny weekend afternoons Fido and Rover sit happily on the deck next to the pool.

   Adjective(s):

   Adverb(s):

4. Quietly, he crept through the extremely scary forest.

   Adjective(s):

   Adverb(s):

5. The boy in the blue shorts never runs very fast around the track.

   Adjective(s):

   Adverb(s):

Part 1: What questions do <u>adverbs</u> answer?

_____ , _____ & _____

Part 2: What kinds of words do <u>adjectives</u> describe?

_____ & _____

Part 3: What kinds of words do <u>adverbs</u> describe?

_____ , _____ & _____

Part 4: Analyzing Sentences

Use "The Routine":

> **First,** surround prepositional phrases with parentheses.
> **Second,** mark the verb(s) with a box (action verb) or an "L" shape (linking verb).
> **Third,** circle the subject(s).
> **Then and only then,** identify adjectives and adverbs—mark ADJ and ADV.

1. Before the party Joseph slept quietly on the couch in the living room.

2. The horse in that barn may gallop through the pasture later.

3. The mother and daughter have never been shopping at the mall.

4. In the winter, birds look for food under the bright white snow.

5. The burn on my arm was gradually caused by the sun.

6. In the middle of the night fire trucks are always sitting quietly in the

firehouses around our town.

7. Everyone on the dock had been in the lake yesterday.

8. That woman should not be walking in the park alone.

Evaluation 7: The Questions Adverbs Answer + Recognizing Adverbs and Adjectives – Are you ready now?

Pun
Fun

Bulldozer

Some Adverb Clues

A. You may have noticed that a lot of adverbs have the same "-ly" ending. It's true; **many "-ly" words are in fact adverbs—but not all "-ly" words are adverbs**, so be careful.

B. Remember, if it's an adverb, it's answering one of the adverb questions: Where? When? or How?

Examples:

> After the leisurely walk we were **totally** relaxed. (*How* relaxed were they?)

> The friendly man **happily** ate his pizza. (*How* did the man eat his pizza?)

<u>Adjectives</u> describe nouns and pronouns. Above, *leisurely* and *friendly* are adjectives because they both describe nouns. <u>Adverbs</u> NEVER describe nouns or pronouns.

C. Remember that the words "polluting" verb phrases are adverbs!

Examples:

> I will **never** speed in my new sports car! (*When* will you speed? *Never.*)

> My friend has **completely** disappointed me. (*How* has your friend disappointed you? *Completely.*)

D. There are also some words that are ALWAYS adverbs. You might refer to these as "classic" adverbs—they are VERY common!

"Classic" Adverbs	
not	very
never	really
already	too
almost	soon
also	

E. Finally, *(and this is a lame-sounding strategy but it just goes to show how difficult adverbs can be)* if you're having real trouble figuring out what part of speech a word is, **you're probably looking at an adverb!!**

Exercise 23

Part 1: Surround prepositional phrases with parentheses. One or two sentences have no prepositional phrases. (You will use the blank line after each sentence for Part 4 of this practice sheet.)

1. On the bus David handed me a <u>dark</u> green sweatshirt. _____

2. You and Brian will always be my fiercest <u>competitors</u>. _____

3. The captain of the <u>fishing</u> boat gives his orders forcefully. _____

4. My brother keeps his tiny bedroom <u>extremely</u> clean. _____

5. Over the weekend Susan and Janis studied very <u>hard</u>

for Monday's quiz and Tuesday's test. _____

6. We became really <u>sleepy</u> during the long bus ride. _____

7. To my dad and me hot dogs at the ballpark taste <u>awesome</u>. _____

8. Bob was <u>still</u> in line after three hours of waiting. _____

9. I would <u>not</u> cross a raging river after a huge rain storm. _____

10. That <u>friendly</u> puppy is licking my brother's face. _____

Part 2: In the sentences in Part 1, locate the verbs. Draw a rectangle around action verbs and draw an "L" shape under linking verbs. Do NOT include adverbs that may be "polluting" verb phrases.

Part 3: In the sentences in Part 1, circle the subjects.

Part 4: In the blank after each sentence in Part 1, identify the underlined word as either an adjective (ADJ), predicate adjective (PA), predicate nominative (PN), or adverb (ADV).

Extra Practice for Evaluation 8

Part 1: In the blank after each sentence, identify the underlined word as either an adjective (ADJ), predicate adjective (PA), predicate nominative (PN), or adverb (ADV).

1. Beside the table Tom read <u>quietly</u> under the lamp light. _____

2. He sleepily fell into a dream about a <u>holiday</u> parade. _____

3. The fountain at the park is <u>full</u> of coins. _____

4. The boys in blue were the <u>winners</u> of the tournament. _____

5. <u>Soon</u> the police arrived on the scene. _____

6. During the winter I become <u>very</u> cranky. _____

Part 2: Complete "The Routine" for each sentence **below**, AND write ADV over each adverb. <u>Each sentence has one adverb</u>.

> **First,** surround prepositional phrases with parentheses.
> **Second,** mark the verb(s) with a box (action verb) or an "L" shape (linking verb).
> **Third,** circle the subject(s).
> **Then and only then,** identify adverbs. /

7. Tom's very silvery spandex shirt has been sparkling in the sun.

8. He and his small son were already filled with disappointment.

9. In tears, the little girl tugged softly on her mother's dress.

10. From the horizon the sun came up and brightened the room.

11. Tom had slept soundly in the chair under the lamp.

12. He was also rooting for the little boy.

Evaluation 8: Finding Adverbs + Recognizing Adjectives, Predicate Adjectives, and Predicate Nominatives in Sentences – Are you ready now?

Pun Fun

Chapter 5

Dialogue Review, Titles, & Possessive Apostrophes

*You know that sentences begin with capital letters and end with periods, right? Well, when are you going to learn how to **punctuate dialogue**? Dialogue is all over the place! Take notice and let's get this down!!*

*What about **titles**? Every essay you write needs one and every book you read has one—so let's also nail down the rules with capitalizing, underlining, italicizing, etc. for titles once and for all!! The same goes for **possessive apostrophes**!!*

5.1 – Punctuating Dialogue, a Review

A. After each rule, circle the correctly punctuated sentence. Some rules are repeated!

RULES:

Quotations begin with a capital letter.	Pete said, "Hello, Joe."	Pete said, "hello, Joe."
You need punctuation at the end of a quotation.	"Please go" said Joe.	"Please go," said Joe.
You need a comma before a quotation.	Pete said, "I am."	Pete said "I am."
Punctuation goes inside the quotation mark.	"I am"? asked Joe.	"I am?" asked Joe.
Before you say who said it, do not use a period.	"I am." said Pete.	"I am," said Pete.
Punctuation goes inside the quotation mark.	"No way", said Joe.	"No way," said Joe.
Words like said, exclaimed, and asked are NEVER capitalized.	"I am!" Exclaimed Pete.	"I am!" exclaimed Pete.
You need punctuation at the end of a quotation.	"Yes way," said Joe.	"Yes way" said Joe.
Punctuation goes inside the quotation mark.	Pete asked, "Are we done yet"?	Pete asked, "Are we done yet?"
Interrupted sentences in quotations have a comma and small letter in the middle.	"I am," said Joe, "and so are you."	"I am," said Joe, "And so are you."
Words like said, exclaimed, and asked are NEVER capitalized.	"Who knew?" said Pete.	"Who knew?" Said Pete.
When "said ____" is between sentences, end with a period and restart with a capital letter.	"I did," said Joe. "You're nuts."	"I did," said Joe, "you're nuts."
Punctuation goes inside the quotation mark.	"No way," said Pete.	"No way", said Pete.
You need punctuation at the end of a quotation.	"Please go" said Joe.	"Please go!" said Joe.

B. When you have two or more speakers, change to a new paragraph when you switch to a different speaker. (Yes, dialogue makes for some mighty small paragraphs!):

Joe said, "Why don't we go get something to eat down at the deli?"

"Sure," Pete replied. The boys then hopped on their bikes and headed down the street. Pete suddenly yelled, "Watch out!"

"What?" said Joe, and then a giant bunny stepped on him.

"I'm not hungry anymore," said Pete.

"Over here!" shouted someone nearby.

"Where?" said Pete.

"Right here," they said. Pete looked toward the sidewalk. Joe was OK!

"Dude, that bunny was made of marshmallow!" said Joe. "Want a bite?"

(Go ahead and add a few more lines of dialogue if you think you know what you're doing!)

_____

_____

_____

_____

_____

_____

Remember: Two different speakers are **NOT** allowed to speak in the <u>same</u> paragraph.

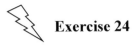 **Exercise 24**

Directions: Find 10-12 lines in a novel that have lots of dialogue. Copy the dialogue below exactly as it appears in the book—paragraph indentations, commas, capital letters, etc. **Copy it perfectly** and think about the rules involved with punctuating, capitalizing, and paragraphing dialogue.

_____

_____

_____

_____

_____

_____

_____

_____

_____

_____

_____

_____

_____

_____

_____

_____

_____

_____

Advanced Exercise A

Directions: Write the letter of the perfectly punctuated, capitalized, and paragraphed line or dialogue, **AND circle each area where you see an error.**

_____ **1.**

A. "Of all the stories in this book," the teacher said, "which do you like the least? Choose only one".

B. "Of all the stories in this book," the teacher said, "Which do you like the least? Choose only one."

C. "Of all the stories in this book," the teacher said. "Which do you like the least? Choose only one."

D. "Of all the stories in this book," the teacher said, "which do you like the least? Choose only one."

_____ **2.**

A.   Jim leaped onto the desk and shouted, "Come on!" There was thunder in his voice, but the other students were unsure of what to do.
     "Wait a second." Said Bobby.
     "Yeah," said Mary, "You're acting crazy. That sound isn't a fire alarm—it's the bell to begin class!"

B.   Jim leaped onto the desk and shouted, "Come on!" There was thunder in his voice, but the other students were unsure of what to do.
     "Wait a second," said Bobby.
     "Yeah," said Mary, "you're acting crazy. That sound isn't a fire alarm—it's the bell to begin class!"

C.   Jim leaped onto the desk and shouted, "Come on". There was thunder in his voice, but the other students were unsure of what to do.
     "Wait a second." Said Bobby.
     "Yeah," said Mary, "You're acting crazy. That sound isn't a fire alarm—it's the bell to begin class!"

D.   Jim leaped onto the desk and shouted, "Come on!" There was thunder in his voice, but the other students were unsure of what to do.
     "Wait a second," said Bobby. "Yeah," said Mary, "You're acting crazy. That sound isn't a fire alarm—it's the bell to begin class!"

_____ **3.**

A. "Are you coming?" asked Tom, "You need to get on the bus right away."
B. "Are you coming?" asked Tom, "you need to get on the bus right away."
C. "Are you coming?" asked Tom. "You need to get on the bus right away."
D. "Are you coming?", asked Tom. "You need to get on the bus right away."

_____ **4.**

A.   "I love cake," said Tom.

"Me, too," replied Janice. Janice then went to the cupboard to see if there was any chocolate cake mix on the shelf. She didn't see any.

"Darn," she said.

"What's wrong?" Said Tom.

"We're out of cake mix," said Janice. She began to cry. Tom came over and sat beside her. He began to laugh. "What's so funny?" Said Janice.

"We're being ridiculous about a stupid cake!" Said Tom.

"You're right. Let's have cookies instead," said Janice. That day, Tom and Janice baked three dozen delicious chocolate chip cookies. It was the most wonderful day of their lives.

B.   "I love cake" said Tom.

"Me, too." replied Janice. Janice then went to the cupboard to see if there was any chocolate cake mix on the shelf. She didn't see any. "Darn" she said.

"What's wrong?" said Tom.

"We're out of cake mix" said Janice. She began to cry. Tom came over and sat beside her. He began to laugh. "What's so funny?" said Janice.

"We're being ridiculous about a stupid cake!" said Tom.

"You're right. Let's have cookies instead." said Janice. That day, Tom and Janice baked three dozen delicious chocolate chip cookies. It was the most wonderful day of their lives.

C.   "I love cake," said Tom.

"Me, too," replied Janice. Janice then went to the cupboard to see if there was any chocolate cake mix on the shelf. She didn't see any. "Darn," She said.

"What's wrong?" Said Tom.

"We're out of cake mix," Said Janice. She began to cry. Tom came over and sat beside her. He began to laugh. "What's so funny?" said Janice.

"We're being ridiculous about a stupid cake!" Said Tom.

"You're right. Let's have cookies instead," Said Janice. That day, Tom and Janice baked three dozen delicious chocolate chip cookies. It was the most wonderful day of their lives.

D.   "I love cake," said Tom.

"Me, too," replied Janice. Janice then went to the cupboard to see if there was any chocolate cake mix on the shelf. She didn't see any. "Darn," she said.

"What's wrong?" said Tom.

"We're out of cake mix," said Janice. She began to cry. Tom came over and sat beside her. He began to laugh. "What's so funny?" said Janice.

"We're being ridiculous about a stupid cake!" said Tom.

"You're right. Let's have cookies instead," said Janice. That day, Tom and Janice baked three dozen delicious chocolate chip cookies. It was the most wonderful day of their lives.

_____ 5.

    A. "I don't know," Louise said, "if he will be there."
    B. "I don't know," Louise said, "If he will be there."
    C. "I don't know," Louise said. "If he will be there."
    D. "I don't know," Louise said. "if he will be there."

_____ 6.

    A. My mother always said, "Haste makes waste."
    B. My mother always said, "Haste makes waste".
    C. My mother always said, "haste makes waste."
    D. My mother always said "Haste makes waste."

_____ 7.

    A. My mom asked, "did you clean your room today?"
    B. My mom asked, "Did you clean your room today"?
    C. My mom asked "Did you clean your room today?"
    D. My mom asked, "Did you clean your room today?"

SCHOLAR ZONE

Some English Etymology

English is a language that includes many words that were born out of a combination of other northern European languages.

"Etymology" means the study of the origin of words and the way a word's meaning has changed over time.

    For example, look at the etymology of the word "eat":

- For the Goths (an ancient northern European tribe) "eat" was **itan.**

- For the Dutch "eat" was (and remains!) **eten.**

- For the Germans "eat" was (and remains!) **essen.**

- In Old English "eat" was **etan.**

Finally, we arrived at the modern version in English: **eat** (the "a" remains as sort of a relic and a connection to the oldest version of the word...)

Once the printing press was invented around 1450, spellings began to become standardized. When the first English dictionary was printed and published around the year 1600, spellings were just about set. That's why Modern English dates back to about the 16th century.

5.2 – Titles: Capitalizing, Italicizing, Underlining, & Using Quotation Marks

A. First, most words in a title get capitalized.

1. Nouns, pronouns, verbs, adjectives, adverbs, and first words ALWAYS get capitalized no matter how short they are!

2. The **only** words that do NOT get capitalized are…

    a. Short prepositions (four letters or less), such as *in*, *to*, *for*, *with*, etc.

        (Longer prepositions <u>do</u> get capitalized, like *about*, *above*, *along*, *under*, *without*, etc.)

    b. Short conjunctions, like *if*, *as*, *but*, *so*, *and*, *or*, etc.

    c. The articles: *a*, *an*, and *the*

3. But remember: The first word in a title ALWAYS gets capitalized.

4. **And the best rule to remember is:** Nouns, pronouns, verbs, adjectives, adverbs, and first words ALWAYS get capitalized no matter how short they are! For other words, short ones are not capitalized.

Two titles below have a capitalization error. Try to find the errors!

The Lord of the Rings

The Fault in our Stars

The Way We Live Now

The Truth About Forever

The Sky Is Everywhere

Three Men in a Boat

It's Not Summer Without You

I am the Messenger

Journey to the End of the Night

The Curious Incident of the Dog in the Night-Time

Alice's Adventures in Wonderland

B. Second, you may have noticed that titles are sometimes <u>underlined</u>, sometimes *italicized*, and sometimes they have "quotation marks around them." What to do when??

    1. Italicize or underline <u>*BIG*</u> things, like novels, textbook titles, and album titles.

        And note: Italicizing and underlining are **equivalent**. When you use a keyboard, italicize or underline. When you write by hand, underline.

    2. Put quotation marks around "smaller" things, like short story and poem titles, chapter titles, and song titles.

    3. Never do *two* things to a title, like underline **and** italicize it or underline **and** put quotation marks around it.

 Exercise 25

<u>**Directions:**</u> Properly capitalize the following titles, and then either surround with quotation marks OR underline each:

(Reminder: Nouns, pronouns, verbs, adjectives, adverbs, and first words ALWAYS get capitalized no matter how short they are! For other words, short ones are not capitalized.)

1. the road not taken (poem) _____

2. chapter one: monkeys (chapter in a textbook) _____

3. a curious kitten (novel) _____

4. dance under the table (song) _____

5. the man who ate the worm (short story) _____

6. pizza dough (chapter in a cookbook) _____

7. the dark side of the moon (musical album title) _____

8. she will be a star (novel) _____

Advanced Exercise B

Companies that publish books, newspapers, magazines, etc. develop their own rules for things like quotation mark usage and capitalizing titles. **Remember:** *The rules in this book apply to* <u>*academic*</u> *writing, and you will from time to time see other rules at work in the novels, magazines, newspapers, etc. that you read.*

Here are some newspaper headlines from two different newspapers:

Headlines from Newspaper A	Headlines from Newspaper B
Poll shows tight Senate race	A Window Into the Real Las Vegas
Shuttle to launch after Mother's Day	Intel Said to Be in Talks to Acquire Rival

<u>**Part 1**</u>: Complete a Venn diagram that compares and contrasts <u>Newspaper A's rules</u> about capitalizing titles with <u>Newspaper B's rules</u>.

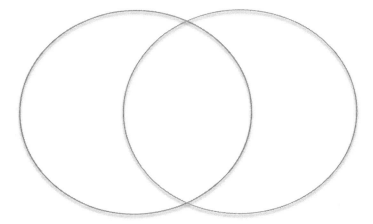

<u>**Part 2**</u>: Newspaper B's rules are more similar to our academic rules. Make a Venn diagram comparing and contrasting <u>Newspaper B's rules</u> about capitalizing titles with <u>our academic rules</u>.

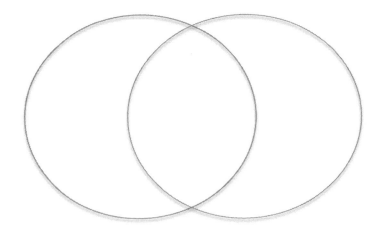

5.3 – Possessive Apostrophes

A. In order to show ownership or possession, in English very often we use something called an *apostrophe "s."*

For example, if you were talking about a jacket owned by Martha, you would write

Martha's jacket

B. Most commonly, apostrophes in English are used to stand in for missing letters or numbers, like below:

'90s   I'll   you're

C. Which brings us to the theory of where the <u>possessive</u> apostrophe came from. Interested?

> If you have been reading the **SCHOLAR ZONE** entries, you now know that English has its roots in Germanic languages. In Old English, as with many German words (especially in older German), *–es* was often added to nouns to show ownership or possession.
>
> For example, in Old English our modern word *boat* was spelled *bat*. Its possessive form was *bates*, which is the equivalent of our word *boat's*.
>
> As English evolved, somewhere along the line, for possessive forms ending in *–es*, an apostrophe began to take the place of the silent "e" of the possessive *–es* ending. So, for instance, *bates* would become *bat's*. This practice caught on!
>
> BTW, how did we get from *bat* in Old English to *boat* in Modern English?? CLUE: In one northern European language (Old Norse) from the region where English developed, *boat* was *batr*. In German, *boat* is *boot*… **What do you think happened?**

D. So, technically, that single apostrophe we use for *apostrophe "s"* situations to show ownership or possession is standing in for some long lost "e"!

Our Modern Possessive Apostrophe Rule

A. GENERAL RULE:

For most nouns, simply add *apostrophe "s"* …

> **unless** BOTH of the following things are true about the word you need to make possessive:

☐ the word ends with an "s"

☐ the word is plural

If neither or only one of the boxes is checked, stick with the very common *apostrophe "s."*

*(If <u>both</u> boxes are checked, then add **just an apostrophe**…)*

Here's another way to think about it: If you're going to add <u>just</u> an apostrophe, which is quite rare, both of the boxes above must be checked.

Examples:

The lead of the **pencil** = pencil's lead

The lights of the **bus** = bus's lights

The clothes of the **babies** = babies' clothes

The yard of **Mr. Granger** = Mr. Granger's yard

Pun Fun

Pi Thon

©Richbaub's Ink Works

B. EXCEPTION #1: <u>Proper</u> Nouns (nouns that must be capitalized)...

If following the General Rule makes it really awkward, then don't follow the General Rule—do what sounds best!

Examples:

A. The plate of **Tess** = Tess**'s** plate

B. The office of **Mr. Collins** = Mr. Collins' office *(breaks the rule)*

C. The sandwich of **Chris** = Chris**'s** sandwich

D. The coastline of **Massachusetts** = Massachusetts' coastline
(breaks the rule)

C. EXCEPTION #2: <u>Personal</u> Pronouns do NOT use *apostrophe "s."* They have built-in possessive forms:

I/me= **my, mine**   we/us = **our, ours**
you = **your, yours**   they/them = **their, theirs**
he/him/she/her/it = **his, her, hers, its**   *who/whom = **whose**

*technically, *whose, who,* and *whom* are not personal pronouns—but they behave so much like personal pronouns that it's helpful to think of them as belonging to this group

The bold words above represent a *third* case of Personal Pronouns, the **possessive case** (in addition to the objective and nominative cases).

Personal pronouns are the **only** pronouns that have special forms that show possession. <u>Other pronouns follow the regular *apostrophe "s"* rule.</u>

Examples: (all italicized words are pronouns in possessive forms)

everyone's homework   (indefinite pronoun)

our tent   (possessive personal pronoun, no *apostrophe "s"*)

that phone is *hers*   (possessive personal pronoun, no *apostrophe "s"*)

its job   (possessive personal pronoun, no *apostrophe "s"* – BTW, *it's* means "it is"!)

another's toothbrush   (indefinite pronoun)

whose lunch   (possessive personal pronoun, no *apostrophe "s"* – BTW, *who's* means "who is"!)

SCHOLAR ZONE

A Few Words with Interesting Etymologies

Lunatic
On a full moon, legend has it, werewolves come out! Full moons have been blamed for all sorts of nutty behavior, so the Latin (Roman) word for moon, *luna*, is the root of *lunatic*, which means "someone who is either clinically insane or just acting really crazy" (vocabulary.com). *BONUS:* Do you know why a "luna moth" is so named?

Jeans
The type of cotton fabric used for jeans was first spun in Genoa, Italy. Centuries ago, the French referred to Genoa as Jannes. As far back as the 15th century, this special fabric from Jannes/Genoa was referred to as "jeans cotton." Do you see the connection between the words Genoa, Jannes, and *jeans*?

Nightmare
In Old English the word *mare* meant "monster," especially a monster like a goblin or demon that came out at night to terrorize its victims in their beds. So *nightmare* originally meant "night monster." It's not hard to see then how that connects with our current definition of *nightmare*: a bad dream that's seriously scary or upsetting, or something terrible that happens any time, even when you're awake (paraphrased from vocabulary.com).

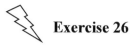 **Exercise 26**

Directions: For each of the following, re-arrange the words so that you have to use a possessive apostrophe. (The **bold** word is the word that will/will not get the apostrophe/*apostrophe "s."*)

Ex: *the shoes of the **boy***   *the boy's shoes*

1. the hairbrush of **Danielle**   _____

2. the sweatshirt of a **kid**   _____

3. the roof of **it**   _____

4. the comb of **someone**   _____

5. the sneakers of the **women**   _____

6. the baseball of **Charles**   _____

7. the part for the **actress**   _____

8. the sketchpad of the **artist**   _____

9. the shopping cart of **them**   _____

10. the gloves of the **girls**   _____

Chapter 6

Sentence Dissecting

Sentence dissecting forces you to look at sentences super closely, like they're some kind of creature you are dissecting. It's a fun way to help you review everything you've learned so far about grammar in a more graphic way than just circling and underlining things in a sentence.

Guess what? There's no formaldehyde involved, and you won't be pulling apart dead worms or frogs! Sentence dissecting is much cleaner, my friends. You simply draw a little chart and pull each word from the sentence and carefully place it on the chart.

Sentence dissecting will especially help you get a deeper understanding of adjectives and adverbs and even introduce you to adjective and adverb phrases—whole groups of words that together work as descriptive forces within a sentence.

6.1 – An Introduction to Sentence Dissecting

A. Sentence dissecting, also called "sentence diagramming," is when you draw lines that connect to each other, and on each line you put a different word from a sentence.

B. Here's an example sentence on a "dissection chart":

On Sunday Josephine swam in the pool for three hours.

C. Here's another:

Josephine became quite wrinkled.

D. If you're already pretty good at labeling the parts of a sentence, learning to dissect sentences isn't too hard—you just need to learn where the parts fit on a dissection chart, which is what the next couple of pages are all about. **Do the next two pages along with your teacher. ***

*You can also check the appendix to see the answers! See p. 151.

How to Chart...	Examples:
Subjects and verbs	1. Maria read.
Verb phrases	2. Thomas should have been studying.
Words that "pollute" verb phrases	3. Trains have not arrived.
Compound subjects (more than one subject)	4. Jonas and Ryan are running.
Compound verbs (more than one verb)	5. Emily ate and drank.
Adjectives	6. The tall men are eating.

Predicate adjectives	7. The boys became noisy.
Adverbs	8. The short girls were swimming quickly.
Predicate nominatives	9. That woman is a terrific doctor.
Prepositional phrases	10. Joe went to the game.
	11. The boy down the street is running in circles.
	12. I often run at the park near my house.

Exercise 27

Directions: Make a dissection chart for each of the following sentences:

1. Birds will often sit on the mailbox.

2. Three cows mooed at the moon.

3. Some of the girls may be sleeping.

4. I am very nervous about the championship game!

5. Weeds and rocks clung to the hillside near the brook.

6.2 – Adjective & Adverb Phrases

A. Yes, prepositional phrases are actually descriptive things. As a matter of fact, many people refer to them simply as Adjective and Adverb Phrases, depending on what they're doing in a sentence.

B. Can you find the Adjective Phrase in the sentence below? *(**Hint:** the prepositional phrase describing a noun or pronoun.)*

The tent in my backyard is ready for our campout.

Your answer: _____

C. There's also an Adverb Phrase in the sentence above. *(**Hint:** the prepositional phrase answering When? Where? or How? about a verb, adjective, or adverb.)* What is it?

Your answer: _____

D. Deciding if prepositional phrases are Adjective or Adverb Phrases can be trickier than finding plain old adjectives and adverbs. For instance, in the example sentence above, doesn't it kind of seem like "in my backyard" answers the adverb question *Where?*

E. In order to avoid confusion, it helps to know what questions <u>adjectives</u> answer. Every adjective, as well as every Adjective Phrase, answers one of the following questions:

Which one?	…the man *on the skateboard*
What kind?	…the donuts *with jelly filling*
How much?	…quality *above the rest*
How many?	…bagels *by the dozen*

F. Back to the example sentence:

The tent **in my backyard** is ready for our campout.

Do you see which <u>adjective</u> question "in my backyard" answers about the tent? Write the question below:

_____

G. One more thing: <u>Adverb</u> Phrases (unlike regular adverbs) can also answer *Why?*, so adverb phrases answer:

When?   Where?   How?   *or*   Why?

For example:

I am shopping for my brother's birthday. (shopping *why?*)
I run at night. (run *when?*)
We have been studying in the library. (have been studying *where?*)
Susan took the quiz with a black pen. (took *how?*)

H. Recap:

Adjective Phrases describe nouns and pronouns and answer…	**Adverb Phrases** describe verbs, adjectives, and adverbs and answer…
Which one? What kind? How much? How many?	When? Where? How? Why?

Exercise 28

Directions: In the blank to the right of each sentence label the underlined prepositional phrase ADV or ADJ. **Hint:** It will be helpful to know what questions adverbs answer and what questions adjectives answer.

1. We will be in Michigan <u>on Wednesday</u>.   _____

2. The dog <u>on her lap</u> is sleeping soundly.   _____

3. A career in medicine is attractive <u>to me</u>.   _____

4. The peanut butter is in the cupboard <u>next to the crackers</u>.   _____

5. A camel might spit on the man <u>in front of me</u>!   _____

6. You should drink some water <u>before the race</u>.   _____

7. The joggers <u>on the sidewalk</u> are moving slowly.   _____

8. The sweater with stripes <u>in the drawer</u> was made by her.   _____

P.S – How would you chart an adverb describing an adjective or adverb? Here's how:

A. The tiger ate quite slowly.   B. The very long ride was terrible!

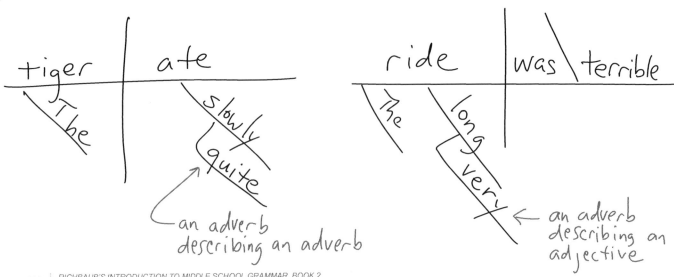

Adjective/Adverb Phrases & Sentence Dissecting Charts

A. Sentence dissecting can come in handy when you're trying to tell if a prepositional phrase is an Adjective Phrase or an Adverb Phrase.

B. If you're dissecting a sentence and you put a prepositional phrase under a noun or pronoun, guess what? It must be an Adjective Phrase since it's describing a noun or pronoun.

Example:

The mouse near the trashcan is looking at me.

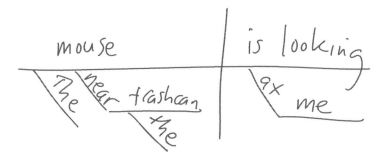

Above, "near the trashcan" is an Adjective Phrase since it's describing the noun *mouse*. Only adjectives describe nouns such as *mouse*! (In case you're wondering, the phrase is answering "Which one?" [Which *mouse* is looking at me?])

C. And so it follows that if you find a prepositional phrase that goes under a *verb*, *adjective*, or *adverb*, then it must be an Adverb Phrase. In the blank line below, write the Adverb Phrase from the dissection chart above:

_____

(Which adverb question is this phrase answering?)

Exercise 29

Part 1: Create a dissection chart for each sentence.

1. The man on the news is serious.

2. The halfbacks and the linebackers are exercising before the game.

3. The walrus at the zoo seems upset with its trainers.

4. She and I will never swim in the pool with her.

Part 2: Answer the following questions about the sentences above.

    A. In sentence # 1 is "on the news" an adjective or adverb phrase? _____

    B. In sentence # 2 is "before the game" an adjective or adverb phrase? _____

    C. In sentence # 3 is "with its trainers" an adjective or adverb phrase? _____

    D. In sentence # 4 is "with her" an adjective or adverb phrase? _____

The Bottom Line About Placing Prepositional Phrases in a Sentence Dissection Chart

A. The most difficult thing about dissecting sentences is putting prepositional phrases in the right spot. However, there are a few things to remember that can make charting prepositional phrases easier.

1. Prepositional phrases at the very beginning of sentences ALWAYS go under the verb. (If you think about this for a moment, you'll realize that ALL prepositional phrases that begin sentences are therefore Adverb Phrases.)

2. <u>Most</u> other prepositional phrases will go under the word <u>right before them</u>. Not all of them will, but *most* of them will. Have you noticed this pattern?

3. If a prepositional phrase doesn't seem to fit under the word right before it, make a *thoughtful, logical* choice. What makes the most sense? What was the author's purpose in placing that prepositional phrase where he or she did? And don't forget to think about <u>the kinds of words adjective and adverb phrases describe and the questions they answer</u>!

B. **One More Important Reminder:** Words polluting verb phrases ALWAYS go under the verb.

Quick Practice

Create a dissection chart for each of the following sentences.

1. From my porch I looked across the street at my neighbor's flowers.

2. The children under the parachute are still giggling.

Exercise 30

Part 1: In the box after each sentence, put an "A" if the sentence's verb is Action and an "L" if the verb is Linking, then dissect each sentence.

1. The wishing well at the castle was built with rocks from a wizard's quarry. ☐

2. For most people the shadows of trees can look really scary on moonlit nights. ☐

3. The boys on that team will usually practice on Saturday afternoons. ☐

4. She and Terrance were always nice to us at the park. ☐

Part 2: Answer the following questions about the sentences above.

    A. In sentence # 1 is "at the castle" an adjective or adverb phrase? _____

    B. In sentence # 2 is "for most people" an adjective or adverb phrase? _____

    C. In sentence # 3 is "on that team" an adjective or adverb phrase? _____

    D. In sentence # 4 is "to us" an adjective or adverb phrase? _____

SCHOLAR ZONE

Anagrams

An anagram is a word or phrase that is formed out of the letters of another word or phrase.

For instance, an anagram of the word *persist* is *stripes*. Anagrams can be clever, funny, or spooky:

funeral = real fun   the eyes = they see

clothes pin = So, let's pinch!   decimal point = I'm a dot in place.

Have you read any of the books in the *A Series of Unfortunate Events* series by Lemony Snicket? If you have, maybe you noticed that some of the characters' names are anagrams of the eccentric bad guy, Count Olaf, such as:

Al Funcoot in *The Bad Beginning*

Dr. Lucafront in *The Reptile Room*

Foreman Flacutono in The Miserable Mill

Nurses Tocuna and Flo in *The Hostile Hospital*

A fun and easy way to make anagrams is to use the letter tiles from a Scrabble board game. **Spell out your name with the game tiles, then rearrange the tiles to see what kinds of anagrams you can make for your name!**

If you can't get a hold of a Scrabble game, cut out the letters of your name below and get to it!

A	B	C	D	E	F	G	H	I	J	K	L	M
N	O	P	Q	R	S	T	U	V	W	X	Y	Z
A	B	C	D	E	F	G	H	I	J	K	L	M
N	O	P	Q	R	S	T	U	V	W	X	Y	Z
A	B	C	D	E	F	G	H	I	J	K	L	M
N	O	P	Q	R	S	T	U	V	W	X	Y	Z
A	B	C	D	E	F	G	H	I	J	K	L	M
N	O	P	Q	R	S	T	U	V	W	X	Y	Z

Chapter 7

Complements

Wow! You made it to the final chapter! You have one more important concept to learn in order to complete your writer's foundation in grammar. Here we go...

There are three main parts of a sentence: the Subject, the Verb (a.k.a. the Predicate), and the Complement.* Everything else in a sentence is, technically, just decorative.

In many parts of this book, we have generally avoided using sentences with Complements, and so please note that while every sentence does have a Subject and a Verb, not all sentences have Complements; however, Complements are very common. Complements come after verbs, and they <u>complete</u> the meaning of the sentence, which is why they're called Complements.

In addition to introducing you to the terms "direct object" and "indirect object," which are terms common to the study of many languages, a study of Complements will also complete your knowledge of the rules about personal pronoun usage (when to use "I" vs. when to use "me," etc.)

7.1 – Introduction to Complements

A. You actually already know about two kinds of Complements: **Predicate Adjectives** and **Predicate Nominatives**--these are the Complements often found **in <u>linking</u> verb sentences**.

B. Action verb sentences can have Complements, too.

C. The Complements **in <u>action</u> verb sentences** are called **Direct Objects** and **Indirect Objects**.

D. First, let's review Predicate Adjectives and Predicate Nominatives.

*see appendix for some technicalities regarding the term *Predicate*

7.2 – Complements in Linking Verb Sentences: Predicate Adjectives & Predicate Nominatives*

Review Time!

A. Predicate Adjectives and Predicate Nominatives are found after <u>linking</u> verbs. They reach back over the verb to describe the subject. Remember?

B. Predicate Nominatives are nouns and pronouns while Predicate Adjectives are adjectives.

C. Take a look at some examples:

My mother is a nurse. (*Nurse* is a Predicate <u>Nominative</u>.)

The men were angry. (*Angry* is a Predicate <u>Adjective</u>.)

In the carriage the baby seemed really happy. (*Happy* is a Predicate <u>Adjective</u>.)

At eighteen Thomas became the captain of a fishing boat. (*Captain* is a Predicate <u>Nominative</u>.)

D. By the way, Predicate Adjectives and Predicate Nominatives are NEVER found inside Prepositional Phrases!

E. Some sentences do not have a Complement, so some linking verb sentences will have neither a Predicate Adjective nor a Predicate Nominative.

F. Linking verb sentences <u>without</u> a Predicate Adjective or Predicate Nominative:

Jonathan was in the library after school.

My dad has never been on a roller coaster in his entire life.

* see appendix for more information about these terms

Predicate Nominatives & Personal Pronoun Usage

A. Do you remember that there are rules about using Personal Pronouns as Predicate Nominatives?

B. Once again, here are those moody Personal Pronouns:

Personal Pronoun Refresher Box

Objective Case Personal Pronouns	Nominative Case Personal Pronouns
me	I
you	you
her	she
it	it
him	he
us	we
them	they
whom	who

As you can see, *you* and *it* are <u>all-purpose</u> personal pronouns.

C. **For Predicate Nominatives, you may <u>only</u> use Nominative Case Personal Pronouns.** Get it? *Nominative* Case for Predicate *Nominatives*? Pretty clever, huh?

Examples:

This is **she**.

The spies could possibly be **she** and **he**.

©Richbaub's Ink Works

The winner is **who**?

The stars of the concert were Matt and **I**.

The players I admire most are **she** and Mary.

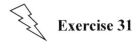 **Exercise 31**

<u>Part 1:</u> Complete "The Routine" for each sentence below.

> **First,** surround prepositional phrases with parentheses.
> **Second,** mark the verb(s) with a box (action verb) or an "L" shape (linking verb).
> **Third,** circle the subject(s).

1. The puppy in the park seems totally lost.

2. I have been in the library for two hours.

3. This soup in my lunchbox tastes really terrible.

4. You should not be on the field during the game.

5. On Halloween I became frightened at the spooky house

on Elm Street.

6. A fire truck was racing through the traffic at rush hour.

7. The players next to me were Brian and he.

8. In the 1950's and 1960's Willie Mays was a terrific baseball player

for the Giants.

9. To Bob and me the picture on that wall looks crooked.

<u>Part 2:</u> In the sentences **above**, over each complement, write PN (Predicate Nominative) or PA (Predicate Adjective). Some sentences will **not** have a complement.

<u>Part 3:</u> Circle the correct Personal Pronouns.

10. The players with the most home runs are (he, him) and Jose.

11. In the front will be Tina, Maureen and (her, she).

12. To Tom and (me, I) the counselors at camp have been awesome.

Exercise 32

Part 1: Choose the correct personal pronoun and make a dissection chart for each of the following sentences.

1. The winners of the race were she and (I , me).

2. The gifts from Joe and (I , me) have been placed under the tree.

3. Joseph and (them , they) were cooking on a propane grill.

4. Mary and (he , him) are always studying for English tests.

Part 2: Answer the following questions about the sentences above.

    A. In sentence # 1 is "of the race" an ADJ or ADV phrase?   _____

    B. In sentence # 2 is "under the tree" an ADJ or ADV phrase?   _____

    C. In sentence # 3 is "on a propane grill" an ADJ or ADV phrase?   _____

    D. In sentence # 4 is "for English tests" an ADJ or ADV phrase?   _____

7.3 – Complements in Action Verb Sentences: Direct Objects & Indirect Objects*

A. Just like Linking Verb sentences, Action Verb sentences can have Complements, too. Complements in <u>Action Verb sentences</u> are called **Direct Objects** and **Indirect Objects**.

B. Direct and Indirect Objects (DO's and IO's) have some similarities with the other Complements, Predicate Adjectives and Predicate Nominatives (PA's and PN's):

    1. They are NEVER found inside Prepositional Phrases.

    2. They typically come after the verb.

C. ALL of these things (DO's, IO's, PA's, and PN's) are Complements, but what are the big <u>differences</u> between them?

    1. DO's and IO's come after **action verbs**. PA's and PN's come after **linking verbs**.

    2. PA's and PN's **describe the subject** of the sentence. DO's and IO's do **NOT** describe the subject of the sentence.

D. Look at the following sentences and notice the similarities and differences between the various kinds of Complements. The first sentence has a PN, the second a PA, the third a DO, and the fourth sentence has a DO *and* an IO. All of these Complements are underlined.

    1. He has been a <u>doctor</u> for sixteen years.

    2. Mary is quite <u>nervous</u> about the math exam.

    3. Before desert you must eat your <u>vegetables</u>.

    4. My dad told <u>us</u> a really boring <u>story</u> at bedtime!

E. Direct and Indirect Objects are both <u>always</u> Nouns or Pronouns. In English, all <u>objects</u> are nouns and pronouns, from *objects* of prepositions, to *objective* case pronouns, to direct and indirect *objects*.

* **see appendix for more information about these terms**

F. Direct Objects are FAR more common than Indirect Objects, and so our discussion of Complements in action verb sentences will first focus on Direct Objects.

P.S. — How would you chart an Adverb Phrase describing an adjective or adverb? Here's how:

We walked silently on our tiptoes.

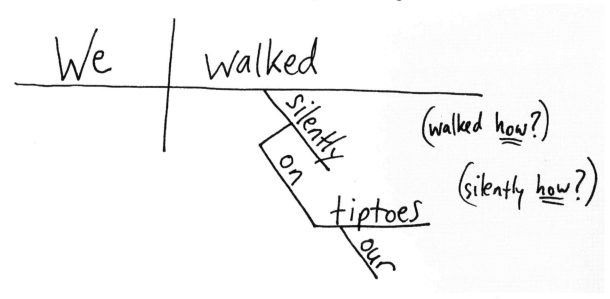

P.S.S. — **Don't forget about sentence dissecting; it's coming back soon!**

In order to stay fresh, give this sentence a try (dissect it!):

In the fish tank near my bed the skittish crab often runs under a conch shell.

Direct Objects

A. In order to find Direct Objects, there is a little trick you can use. Remember, though, to **only look for Direct Objects if the sentence has an action verb!** Here's the trick:

Plug the sentence's subject & verb into this question:

"_____ _____ who or what?"
　　　subject　　　verb

B. Does this look familiar? It's the <u>same</u> trick you can use to find Predicate Adjectives and Predicate Nominatives (see p. 63). Compare the following sentences. The first has a PA, the second a DO:

1. With her friends Mary seemed comfortable.

    "Mary seemed <u>who or what?</u>" complement = _____

2. I washed the dishes after dinner.

    "I washed <u>who or what?</u>" complement = _____

C. Remember, though—**Predicate Adjectives and Predicate Nominatives are only in <u>linking</u> verb sentences while Direct Objects are only found in <u>action</u> verb sentences.**

D. Another Direct Object example:

The policemen washed their cars on Saturday.

Take your subject, *policemen*, and your verb, *washed*, and ask "who or what?"

"<u>Policemen washed</u> who or what?" complement = _____

<u>Since this is an</u> **action verb sentence**, the answer (*cars*) is a Direct Object!

E. More examples of action verb sentences with Direct Objects:

1. The miners blasted a large hole in the wall of the tunnel.

In the sentence above, _____ is a Direct Object.

2. The puppy in the window chewed a rubber toy.

In the sentence above, _____ is a Direct Object.

3. Under the water you can see several species of fish.

In the sentence above, _____ is a Direct Object.

F. Many action verb sentences do <u>not</u> have a Direct Object.

1. Carl thought about the problem for three hours.

2. During gym class on Friday we jogged around the track for 15 minutes.

3. The rain fell quietly on the roof above us.

P.S. — Have you forgotten about sentence dissecting? (How dare you!) To brush up, dissect the sentence below:

The carnival's dunk tank was its most popular attraction.

 **Exercise 33**

Part 1: Follow "The Routine" for each sentence below.

> **First,** surround prepositional phrases with parentheses.
> **Second,** mark the verb(s) with a box (action verb) or an "L" shape (linking verb).
> **Third,** circle the subject(s).

1. The magician at the high school assembly hypnotized my friend!

2. Before a school dance my dad or mom has always washed my favorite jeans for me.

3. Everyone seemed bothered by the smoke from the campfire.

4. That assignment was given to Sheila and me.

5. The lead actors in our school play will be Thomas and I.

6. In the largest cage at the zoo three lions growled at me and my dad.

7. For Lawrence and me this climb may be an impossible challenge.

8. In the swirling wind the umbrella from my table tumbled wildly across the beach.

Part 2: In the sentences in Part 1, over each complement write DO (Direct Object), PN (Predicate Nominative), or PA (Predicate Adjective). Three sentences will **not** have a Complement.

Indirect Objects

A. Action verb sentences can also have Indirect Objects.

B. To look for an Indirect Object, put together a question like so:

Subject + Verb + **Direct Object** + to/for whom, to/for what?

C. Example:

DO
(Sheila gave) me a ride (to the mall.)

"Sheila + gave + ride + ***to or for*** *whom,* ***to or for*** *what?"*

Answer: *"Sheila gave a ride to...* **me**.*"* So *me* is the Indirect Object.

☆ **D. You need to have a Direct Object <u>first</u> in order to have an Indirect Object, so always look for a Direct Object first!**

E. Indirect Objects are pretty rare. It's <u>very</u> common for a sentence to have a DO but no IO.

F. Some more examples:

After dinner my mom brought us a slice of lemon pie.

DO: _____ IO: _____

We built my sister a huge sand castle at the beach on Saturday.

DO: _____ IO: _____

That fifth grade teacher taught her students several multiplication rules.

DO: _____ IO: _____

G. Recognizing patterns in sentences is helpful in grammar—like how the subject usually comes at the beginning of a sentence, the verb usually is in the middle of a sentence, complements typically come after the verb, and how a prepositional phrase will usually describe the word right before it.

Here's one more pattern that's helpful to be aware of:

For DO's and IO's, <u>if you pay attention to patterns</u> (you should!), you'll notice that when there are two nouns (or pronouns) after an action verb, very often the noun (or pronoun) *closest* to the verb is an Indirect Object and the other one is a Direct Object. Look at the following sentences:

               IO   **DO**

1. That movie gives <u>me</u> the <u>creeps</u>!

             IO   **DO**

2. We bought <u>him</u> a <u>bag</u> of lollipops for his birthday.

The only exception to this pattern is when there are <u>two direct objects</u>:

            DO   **DO**

3. The lifeguard saved <u>me</u> and <u>Vanessa</u> from drowning.

H. And remember, some sentences do not have a Complement, so there are action verb sentences that have neither a Direct Object nor an Indirect Object.

Action verb sentences <u>without</u> Complements:

4. The snake slithered under the rocks in the garden.

5. The man behind the counter was laughing at my little joke.

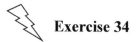 **Exercise 34**

Part 1: In the blank on the left, write the letter of the statement in the box that describes the sentence.

_____ 1. The rain is falling on Tim and I.

_____ 2. My dad and he felt a little sad after the game.

_____ 3. The puppies are having a blast!

_____ 4. Ties can sometimes be difficult to tie.

a. Has a polluted verb phrase
b. Includes a single-word linking verb
c. Has a pronoun case error
d. I see a DO in this sentence.

Part 2: Follow "The Routine" for each sentence below.

        First, surround prepositional phrases with parentheses.
        Second, mark the verb(s) with a box (action verb) or an "L" shape (linking verb).
        Third, circle the subject(s).

5. A long train carried me over the Rocky Mountains toward California.

6. Before bed Charlie always sang his sister a lullaby.

7. In honor of your birthday we will be eating lobster and steak for dinner tonight!

8. The cheetah is a very stealthy hunter on the African plains.

9. The chef cooked Wally a wonderful waffle on Saturday morning.

Part 3: In the sentences in Part 2, above each complement write DO (Direct Object), IO (Indirect Object), PN (Predicate Nominative), or PA (Predicate Adjective). It's possible for a sentence to **not** have a complement.

Part 4: Dissect each of the following sentences.

10. The log cabin is being painted by three mountain men.

11. Your cash for the trip may be in that backpack by the door.

Part 5: *Sentence Puzzles* ✠✠✠ Write sentences as directed.

12. Using the word *throw* as your verb, write a sentence that includes an Indirect Object and a Direct Object. Your sentence should be less than 15 words long.

_____

_____

13. Write a sentence that has just a Direct Object. Your sentence should be less than 12 words long.

_____

_____

14. Write a sentence that has an action verb but NO complement. Your sentence should be less than 12 words long.

_____

_____

15. Write a sentence that has a Predicate Nominative. Your sentence should be less than 12 words long.

_____

_____

Complements, an AV / LV Sort of Thing

Predicate Adjectives　　*Predicate Nominatives*　　*Direct Objects*　　*Indirect Objects*

It's <u>VITAL</u> to understand that...

DO's and IO's are ONLY found in Action Verb sentences,

and that...

PA's and PN's are ONLY found in Linking Verb sentences! Got it?!!

Your Complements Recap

Predicate Adjectives   *Predicate Nominatives*   *Direct Objects*   *Indirect Objects*

The Verb determines what kind of Complement you will have

In Linking Verb sentences	In Action Verb sentences
Look for PA's and PN's (predicate adjectives and predicate nominatives – sometimes called "subject complements")	Look for DO's and IO's (direct objects and indirect objects – sometimes called "object complements")
How to find PA's and PN's	**How to find DO's**

Make a question:
"Subject + Verb + Who or What?"

(For PA's and PN's you can also just look after the linking verb for a word that reaches back and describes the subject.)

In Linking Verb sentences, If answer is a noun or pronoun, you have a **PN** If answer is an adjective, you have a **PA**	*In Action Verb sentences,* Your answer is a **DO**
Tips: - Some sentences do not have any complements - Complements are NEVER found inside prep. phrases - IO's are rare—and you need to have a DO first before you look for an IO	**How to find IO's** Make a question: "S + V + **DO** + to or for whom? to or for what?" Your answer is an **IO**

Exercise 35

<u>Part 1:</u> Follow "The Routine" for each sentence below.

> <u>**First,**</u> surround prepositional phrases with parentheses.
> <u>**Second,**</u> mark the verb(s) with a box (action verb) or an "L" shape (linking verb).
> <u>**Third,**</u> circle the subject(s).

1. The pond in the woods became our hockey rink in January.

2. She asked her a question about the application.

3. The ceremony brought tears to my eyes.

4. Sue and Mary are in the library.

5. This cool weather feels awesome.

6. The coach threw me three curveballs at practice yesterday.

7. At the park we ran away and hid the Frisbee.

8. The boys will go to the mall after dinner.

9. He is not athletic.

10. In other words, that television show is horrible!

11. Everything in the trunk is terribly heavy.

12. After the overtime game the players seemed listless.

13. Those people are walking briskly.

14. The trees were motionless before the storm.

15. The man brought a cake to the party.

<u>Part 2:</u> Label the Complements in the sentences above (DO, IO, PA, or PN). Some sentences will <u>not</u> have any Complements.

Extra Practice for Evaluation 9

Part 1: On the blank line, identify the underlined Complement as a DO, IO, PA, or PN.

1. The players on the team were <u>unhappy</u> about the long practice. _____

2. My mother looks really <u>pretty</u> in the picture on the mantel. _____

3. The doctor delivered the <u>baby</u> at one minute after midnight. _____

4. After college my brother became a <u>lawyer</u> at a downtown office. _____

5. The waitress brought <u>us</u> some straws for our sodas. _____

Part 2: Follow "The Routine" for each sentence below.

> **First,** surround prepositional phrases with parentheses.
> **Second,** mark the verb(s) with a box (action verb) or an "L" shape (linking verb).
> **Third,** circle the subject(s).

6. By Saturday Taryn seemed really excited about the big game.

7. The children became cold at the ballgame.

8. The children usually will eat dinner before sunset.

9. On a warm Sunday she and I ate sandwiches on a blanket in the park.

10. Grandma will tell me that story tomorrow.

11. Some of the people at the beach are sitting under umbrellas.

12. The stars in the nighttime sky became very bright after midnight.

13. This cake tastes extremely good with a glass of cold milk.

Part 3: Label the Complements in the sentences in Part 2 (DO, IO, PA, or PN). Some sentences will <u>not</u> have any Complements.

 Evaluation 9: Complements – Are you ready now?

Pun
Fun

7.4 – Objects & Personal Pronoun Usage

A. We've mentioned Personal Pronouns quite a bit. Do you remember them? If not, here they are once again:

Personal Pronoun Refresher Box

Objective Case Personal Pronouns	Nominative Case Personal Pronouns
me	I
you	you
her	she
it	it
him	he
us	we
them	they
whom	who

As you can see, *you* and *it* are <u>all-purpose</u> personal pronouns.

B. Hopefully you recall that when using Personal Pronouns for Objects of Prepositions (op's), you must use only Objective Case Personal Pronouns.

C. Examples:

For my sister and <u>me</u>, Disney World is the most incredible place on earth.

To <u>whom</u> did you give your pencil?

The ball sailed right **over Sally and <u>him</u>**, and the game was lost.

D. In fact, *all* <u>objects</u> in English are treated the same way.

E. So for Direct and Indirect <u>Objects</u>, as far as Personal Pronouns go, you must also only use <u>Objective</u> Case Personal Pronouns.

F. Examples:

My grandmother bought my **brother** and **<u>me</u>** new **bicycles** yesterday.

The bus will take **<u>us</u>** to the beach after school.

We baked **<u>her</u>** a **cake** on Sunday afternoon.

G. And of course you recall that Personal Pronouns used as Subjects and Predicate Nominatives must be <u>Nominative</u> Case Personal Pronouns.

H. Examples:

My **uncle** and <u>**he**</u> have been hammering away on the dock.

The ones responsible for the damage were <u>**she**</u> and **Tracey**.

<u>**You**</u> and <u>**they**</u> will play for the championship on Saturday night.

I. Here's a recap:

Personal Pronoun Usage Summary

Objective Case Personal Pronouns	Nominative Case Personal Pronouns
me you her it him us them whom **Use for OP's, DO's, & IO's**	I you she it he we they who **Use for Subjects & PN's**
As you can see, *you* and *it* are <u>all-purpose</u> personal pronouns.	

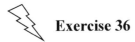 **Exercise 36**

Part 1: Circle the correct personal pronouns.

1. Under the table I gave (her, she) and my brother some of my asparagus.

2. (Her, She) slid the board into the steel blade of the table saw.

3. Tonight's starting pitcher might be Jason or (I, me).

4. (I, Me) and Billy should have some cash left after the movie.

5. The teacher collected the books from Jenny and (me, I).

6. The boys and (we, us) sanded the corners of the shelf.

7. To (who, whom) do you want me to throw the ball?

8. The counselors were discussing bullying with (they, them).

9. My mom and dad should be bringing (her, she) to the game later.

10. That bike crash wounded (he, him) very seriously.

Part 2: Fill in the blanks with <u>personal pronouns</u>.

11. _____ and my dad rode in a hot air balloon in Africa.

12. My teacher assigned Tammy and _____ big roles in the school play.

13. The culprit in the bank scandal was _____ .

14. Bring the donuts to Joe and _____ .

15. For example, between my mom and _____ there are no secrets.

A. On a sentence dissection chart Direct Objects go right **after** the verb. Put a **vertical** line between the Verb and the Direct Object. (Don't use a diagonal line—that's only for PA's PN's!!)

Example:

Jill bought a lollipop.

B. On a sentence dissection chart Indirect Objects go **under** the verb. The line they go on is shaped like the line used for prepositional phrases, but nothing is written on the diagonal line.

Example:

Melinda sold me a house.

Practice:

Gary gave me a cheese pizza.

Exercise 37

Directions: Circle the correct personal pronoun, and then dissect each sentence. DO's, IO's, PA's, and PN's are in some of the sentences but not all of them.

1. For Jim and (I , me) the test was really easy.

2. Everyone is with (he , him) on the bus.

3. (She , Her) and Aunt Mildred picked flowers for Grandma in the afternoon.

4. At the goal line the quarterback tossed (I , me) the football.

5. The people in the audience will be (we , us) and the kids from the beach.

6. The Tigers had you and (me , I) in the backfield on Saturday.

Extra Practice for Evaluation 10

Part 1: Circle the correct answer:

1. Personal pronouns in prepositional phrases are always in the (**objective** , **nominative**) case.

2. Before a verb, *outside of prepositional phrases* choose a/an (**objective** , **nominative**) case personal pronoun.

3. After linking verbs, *outside of prepositional phrases* choose a/an (**objective** , **nominative**) case personal pronoun.

4. After an action verb, always choose a/an (**objective** , **nominative**) case personal pronoun.

Part 2: Circle the correct pronoun.

5. The iced tea without sugar was for Mark and (I, me).

6. The wind blew Diana and (they, them) across the parking lot.

7. With (who, whom) will you be speaking at the bank today?

8. (Me, I) and Sheila just finished a bag of pistachios!

9. (He, him) and his dog frequently walk in the park by my house.

10. Several of the boys helped (we, us) with our chores.

11. The author of that poem is (he, him).

12. Across the hockey rink Johnny slid (me, I) the puck, and I scored!

13. Against all odds, Margo and (we, us) reached the summit of Mt. Fuji.

14. The emperor sat beside my best friend and (I, me)!

Part 3: There are **eight** complements in the sentences above. Label each one.

Part 4: *Sentence Puzzles* ✠✠✠ Write sentences as directed.

15. Begin with a prepositional phrase and include <u>two</u> **personal pronoun** PN's.

_____

_____

16. Use two prepositional phrases and a PA.

_____

_____

17. Use two prepositional phrases, an IO, and a DO. Use "may give" as your verb. Please remember that DO's and IO's are NEVER inside prepositional phrases!

_____

_____

Part 5: Dissect the following sentences.

18. Yesterday Joey and Josh presented the winners huge golden trophies.

19. The bird in this tree chirps loudly at sunrise.

Evaluation 10: Complements and Personal Pronoun Usage – Are you ready now?

(The <u>sentence dissecting</u> on this evaluation will be for bonus points only!)

Pun
Fun

Appendix

A word about the prepositions *after*, *before*, and *until*

Students may become confused at times when dealing with words that appear on their prepositions list that can also be other parts of speech. The preposition *for* is one example of a word that often is a preposition but also can be a conjunction:

The book was <u>for my uncle</u>. (*for* is a preposition)

I woke up extra early, for I did not want to miss the bus on the first day of school. (*For* is a conjunction—a word that, along with a comma, connects two independent clauses to create one compound sentence.)

For is not a big issue since it's mostly used as a preposition and not so much as a conjunction.

The most problematic prepositions that students will encounter are *after* and *before*. These often-used words can also be subordinating conjunctions. When used as subordinating conjunctions, *after* and *before* begin groups of words <u>that also include subjects and verbs</u>. *Until* operates similarly but is less often used by middle school students.

We grabbed a snack <u>before dinner</u>. (*Before* is a preposition.)

I carefully packed my backpack <u>before I left school yesterday</u>. (*Before* is a subordinating conjunction.)

<u>After swim practice</u> we were completely exhausted. (*After* is a preposition.)

<u>After the game ended</u>, fans quickly headed to the stadium's exits. (*After* is a subordinating conjunction.)

The main thing to keep in mind is that prepositional phrases never include verbs.*   If a student creates or marks something that he or she believes to be a prepositional phrase, but something that includes a verb, they may very well be looking at a subordinate clause. Students do this a LOT when making up prepositional phrases that begin with *after* and *before*!

---

*There actually are verb forms in prepositional phrases *sometimes* with more advanced sentence structures. See appendix entry for p. 19 for a discussion of these unique verb forms. Info on p. 146 is most relevant.

Who and *whom* are actually classified as both **interrogative pronouns** (when they begin questions) and **relative pronouns** (when they begin subordinate clauses).

A complete list of the personal pronouns would include the **possessive case personal pronouns**, in addition to the **objective** and **nominative cases**.

POSSESSIVE CASE PERSONAL PRONOUNS	NOTES
my, mine *your, yours* *his* *her, hers* *its* *our* *ours* *their, theirs*	While technically pronouns, these words are typically classified as <u>adjectives</u> (including predicate adjectives*)* when parsing sentences as they answer the adjective question "which one?" about nouns and pronouns. Also notice that *her* appears on this list as well as on the objective case personal pronoun list. In the practice exercises in this book, students trying to use *her* as a pronoun (objective case personal pronoun) often accidentally use *her* as an adjective (possessive case personal pronoun).

The word *being* is often used as a helping verb even though it does not appear in the helping verbs list on p. 19. Here are some sentences where *being* is functioning as a helping verb:

The stamp <u>is being applied</u> to the letter by my sister.

At the gate a suspicious suitcase <u>was being searched</u> by security officers.

However, *being* and other verbs ending in *-ing* can also be classified as participles. Participles, like infinitives (to + verb, see p. 17), are a verb form that behaves differently than traditional verbs.

<u>Participles are verbs ending in *-ing* or *-ed* that actually behave like **adjectives**.</u>

For example:

That crystal <u>serving</u> dish is used only for special holiday meals.

In the sentence above, *serving* describes *dish*, and therefore is a type of adjective called a **participle**. Participles are verb forms behaving like <u>adjectives</u>. *Serving* is a form of the verb "to serve" and it is something one can do, but in this sentence it's functioning as an adjective. The verb in this sentence is "is used."

Another example:

For my birthday I had a triple-decker <u>frosted</u> cake.

In the sentence above, *frosted* describes *cake* and therefore is another example of a verb form acting like an adjective. *Frosted* <u>can</u> be a verb, as in "I frosted the cake," but in the sentence above *frosted* is serving as an adjective. The verb of the sentence is *had*.

Once again, <u>participles</u> are verbs ending in *-ing* or *-ed* that behave like <u>adjectives</u>.

Participles also may begin <u>groups</u> of words that are called **participial phrases**.

For example:

A man <u>staring from the train's window</u> waved at me.

In the sentence above, "staring from the train's window" is what we would call a participial phrase, a group of words that begins with a participle (*staring*) and that, all together, describes a noun (*man*).

It's important for teachers to be aware of participles because <u>students will occasionally create sentences using a participle and wrongly identify the participle as the verb</u>.

For instance:

The little kitten <u>sleeping on the windowsill</u> is so cute!

Above, *is* is the verb. "Sleeping in the windowsill" is a descriptive (adjective) phrase we would call a participial phrase.

Younger middle school students rarely use participial phrases, and so this is not a big issue, just one that a teacher should be aware of.

So far we've mentioned two kinds of verb forms that do not behave like traditional verbs, Participles and infinitives. Participles act like adjectives. Infinitives are a bit more sophisticated, acting like adjectives, nouns, as well as adverbs!

Examples:

In his <u>isolated</u> cabin in the Rocky Mountains my dad loves <u>to paint</u>.

Above, *isolated* is a participle (describing the cabin) and "to paint" is an infinitive. This infinitive is acting as a noun, for it is the <u>thing</u> the dad loves to do. The verb of this sentence is *loves*.

The driver of the <u>speeding</u> car swerved <u>to avoid the telephone pole</u>.

Above, *speeding* is a participle (describing the car) and "to avoid the telephone pole" is an infinitive phrase. This infinitive phrase is acting as an adverb. The verb of the sentence is *swerved*, and the infinitive phrase describes <u>why</u> the car swerved.

Standing in line for movie tickets, I began to chat with a nice lady wearing a fur coat.

Above, "standing in line for movie tickets" is a **participial phrase** (describing *I*) and "to chat with a nice lady wearing a fur coat" is an **infinitive phrase** acting as a noun, for it is the <u>thing</u> the person began to do. Additionally, inside the infinitive phrase is a participial phrase! "Wearing a fur coat" describes the lady. The verb in this sentence is *began*.

Can you imagine a student looking at the sentence above and identifying the verb as "began to chat"? It happens.

Here's a very common mistake students make when directed to compose a sentence that includes a verb phrases:

This jacket seems to be a little too big for me.

Students will consider "seems to be" a verb phrase. Actually, though, "to be a little too big for me" is an infinitive phrase, and the verb for this sentence is the single-word verb *seems*. And, by the way, *seems* (and all of its forms) is **never** a helping verb.

Of course, it has already been mentioned that infinitives are never part of THE verb in a sentences, so technically students should not be including something like "to be" in their verb anyway. However, it does happen.

To come full circle in this very long (but important!) discussion, consider the following sentence:

Joe did not like *being the shortest boy in his class*.

Above, "did like being" is something a student might consider to be the verb. It's not, though; the verb is "did like."

So what is "being the shortest boy in his class"? It certainly <u>looks</u> like a participial phrase, doesn't it?

If you think about it, though, "being the shortest boy in his class" is the THING Joe does not like, and therefore it is…a <u>noun</u> phrase! Such phrases, ones that begin with an *-ing* verb and operate as nouns, are called **gerund phrases**.

Here's a sentence with a single-word **gerund** in it:

<u>Swimming</u> is a great way to cool off in the summertime.

Swimming is the subject of this sentence. No one is doing any swimming and *swimming* is certainly not behaving like a participle here—it's a thing, an activity. Therefore, *swimming* is a gerund.

(Did you notice the infinitive phrase in the sentence?)*

Gerunds and gerund phrases, as well as infinitives and infinitive phrases, may show up in prepositional phrases from time to time, something to watch out for.

Here are some examples:

after eating lunch

(above, the object of the preposition [o.p.] is the gerund phrase "eating lunch")

without stopping

(above, the o.p. is the gerund *stopping*)

about to buy a watch

(above, the o.p. is the infinitive phrase "to buy a watch")

before pushing the button

(above, the o.p. is the gerund phrase "pushing the button")

And so <u>technically</u> it is possible to have a verb inside of a prepositional phrase! Of course, the verb does not behave like a true verb in these circumstances… This is an exception that needs no explanation up front, but it is nice for a teacher to know since students will, from time to time, create such things.

*The infinitive phrase is "to cool off in the summertime."

In conclusion, there are three verb forms that do not behave like verbs:

1. Participles are verb forms ending in either -*ing* or -*ed* that behave like adjectives.
2. Infinitives are "to + a verb" forms that behave like adjectives, nouns, or adverbs.
3. And gerunds are verb forms ending in -*ing* that behave like nouns.

As we have seen in the many examples above, participles, infinitives, and gerunds may be alone or they may begin phrases.

One more factoid: Collectively, participles, infinitives, and gerunds are sometimes called **verbals**. Phew!

Page 27

The verb "to become" is an action verb when it is used to mean *attractive*, as in "That dress is very becoming on you." This definition of the verb "to become" is very infrequently used today.

Page 52

To form the past tense, some verbs in English do not simply get an –*ed* added to them, and this changes their (past) participle form.

	Regular Verb example: "to bake"	**Irregular** Verb example: "to fall"
Present tense	bake	fall
Past tense	baked	**fell**
Present (–*ing*) participle	baking	falling
Past (<u>usually</u> –*ed*) participle	baked	**fallen**

Both verbs above used as participles:

<u>fallen</u> angel   <u>falling</u> tower   <u>baking</u> pan   <u>baked</u> chicken

More irregular past participles in action:

<u>forgotten</u> toys   <u>lost</u> shoe   <u>torn</u> jeans

<u>Page 59 (*)</u>

A **predicate adjective** is a type of subject complement. There are two types of subject complements: predicate adjectives (a.k.a. **adjective complements**) and predicate nominatives (a.k.a. **noun complements**).

<u>Page 59 (**)</u>

At some point students will be confronted with a sentence where it is quite difficult to discern whether one is looking at a verb phrase or a verb + a predicate adjective. For example, consider the following sentence:

The children were excited.

One might consider *excited* to be part of the verb phrase "was excited." After all, *excited* is derived from the verb "to excite," so this makes sense, right?

However, one might also deem *excited* to be a predicate adjective describing the subject, *children*. I mean, *excited* could be a participle (one of those verbs ending in -*ed* that acts as a descriptive word rather than a verb). From this perspective the verb would simply be *was*.

No one needs to lose any sleep over this kind of situation! Either decision is totally acceptable at this level.

What would <u>not</u> be acceptable is if, considering the following sentence, one decided that the verb is "might be powerful."

That engine might be powerful.

In the sentence above, the verb is without a doubt "might be." *Powerful* cannot be part of the verb because *powerful* itself is not a verb.

To dig deeper, let's go back to the original sentence, "The children were excited." Consider how it compares to a similar sentence:

The children were excited. *vs.* The fireworks were exciting.

For each sentence, at the middle school level I would have no problem accepting "were excited"/"were exciting" as the verbs <u>or</u> *were* as the verbs and *excited/exciting* as predicate adjectives.

If you want to get down to the nitty-gritty truth on this issue, however, continue reading. Otherwise, you probably have better things to do!

Here are the sentences again:

1. The children were excited.

2. The fireworks were exciting.

One might argue that in sentence one the children aren't <u>doing</u> anything, that they're just <u>being</u> excited, which is different from sentence two where the fireworks really are doing something, presumably exciting an audience. Such a line of reasoning would lead one to decide that sentence one has a verb (*were*) + a predicate adjective (*excited*) and that sentence two has a verb phrase ("were exciting") and no predicate adjective.

The very best solution when parsing the above sentences, however, is to label "were excited" and "were exciting" <u>both</u> as verb phrases. The only real difference between the two sentences is that sentence one is written in passive voice, while sentence two is written in active voice.

In passive voice sentences, someone or something is in fact doing something—it's just that the <u>subject</u> is not performing the action. For instance, something or someone is exciting the children, it just isn't mentioned. To see this, one needs only to compare the same sentences that have been fleshed out a bit with more information:

A. The children were excited by the fireworks.

B. The fireworks were exciting the children.

Now it is clear that in BOTH sentences someone or something is doing something, exciting the children. Now it is also clear that the verbs are "were excited" and "were exciting" and that there are no predicate adjectives.

A good rule of thumb in these tricky situations is this: If the word in question (in our examples *excited* and *exciting*) is itself a verb, then consider it part of the verb and NOT a predicate adjective.

A final example:

Compare the flowing tricky sentences:

1. The movie will be terrifying.

2. The movie is sad.

In sentence 1, since *terrifying* is a verb (one can <u>terrify</u>, and it is derived from the verb "to terrify"), it will be considered to be part of the verb "will be terrifying," and there is no predicate adjective.

In sentence 2, since *sad* is not a verb (one cannot <u>sad</u>, and it is not derived from any verb form), then it cannot be considered to be part of the verb. Instead, the verb is simply *is*, and *sad* is a predicate adjective.

Technically, the verb is just one part of the predicate and therefore is sometimes referred to as the <u>simple predicate</u>. The <u>complete predicate</u> actually includes the verb, anything describing the verb, and the complement(s) (if any).

Similarly, the subject of a sentence is, technically, the subject **plus** anything describing the subject. The subject alone is therefore sometimes referred to as the <u>simple subject</u>. The <u>complete subject</u> would be the subject plus anything describing the subject. Confusing, huh? Here's an example to clarify:

The birds in the tree squawked loudly at the cat below.

Simple Subject = *birds*   Complete Subject = "The birds in the tree"

Simple Predicate = *squawked*   Complete Predicate = "squawked loudly at the cat below"

For clarity's sake, this book does not use the term "predicate" in reference to verbs. Also, when referring to the subject of a sentence, this book is referring to the subject alone, without descriptors (the simple subject).

Of course, this book does use the terms "predicate adjective" and "predicate nominative." The origin of these terms should now be clear, for they are found inside the predicate (technically the complete predicate) of sentences.

Page 114

Some grammar resources use the term "subject complement" to refer collectively to predicate adjectives and predicate nominatives.

There are two types of subject complements: predicate adjectives (a.k.a. "adjective complements") and predicate nominatives (a.k.a. "noun complements").

Page 118

Direct objects are sometimes called "object complements."

Some grammar resources use the term "object complements" to refer collectively to direct objects and indirect objects.

Other grammar resources use the term "verb complements" to refer collectively to direct objects and indirect objects.

HOW TO DISSECT SENTENCES

How to Chart...	Examples:

Subjects and verbs

1. Maria read.

Maria | read

Verb phrases

2. Thomas should have been studying.

Thomas | should have been studying

Words that "pollute" verb phrases

3. Trains have not arrived.

Trains | have arrived
not

Compound subjects (more than one subject)

4. Jonas and Ryan are running.

Jonas
and
Ryan | are running

Compound verbs (more than one verb)

5. Emily ate and drank.

ate
Emily | and
drank

Adjectives

6. The tall men are eating.

men | are eating
The tall

Predicate adjectives	7. The boys became noisy.

boys | became \ noisy
The

Adverbs	8. The short girls were swimming quickly.

girls | were swimming
The short quickly

ADV + ADJ
look the
same on a
diagram!

Predicate nominatives	9. That woman is a terrific doctor.

woman | is \ doctor
That a terrific

PA + PN's
look the
same, too!

Prepositional phrases	10. Joe went to the game.

Joe | went
to game
the

11. The boy down the street is running in circles.

boy | is running
The down street in circles
the

12. I often run at the park near my house.

I | run
often at park
the near house
my

a prep phrase
may describe
the o.p. of
another prep.
phrase

NOTES

<u>NOTES</u>

<u>NOTES</u>

53603777R00096